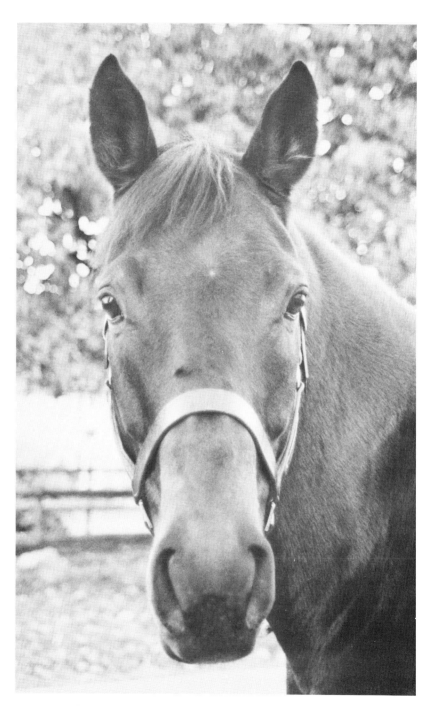

Your best friend.

Dressage
For The Young Rider

Pegotty Henriques

THRESHOLD BOOKS
The Kenilworth Press Limited

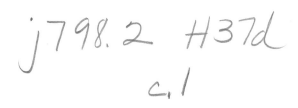

For Nick . . . because.

First published in Great Britain by
Threshold Books, The Kenilworth Press Limited,
661 Fulham Road, London SW6 5PZ
1990

© Text and photographs Pegotty Henriques, 1990

British Library Cataloguing in Publication Data

Henriques, Pegotty
  Dressage for the young rider.
  1. Livestock : Horses. Riding. Dressage
  I. Title
  798.2'3

  ISBN 0–901366–99–4

Typeset by Rapid Communications Ltd., London WC1
Printed and bound in Great Britain by Billing & Sons, Worcester

Contents

CHAPTER ONE

Why Do Dressage?

If you have ridden more than one horse or pony you will know that some horses are nicer or more comfortable to ride than others. This is generally because they are better trained and because they have a walk, trot, and canter that feels pleasant and effortless. If your pony is lazy or naughty it is probably not his fault; he has simply never been taught how to behave properly.

Men have been riding horses for thousands of years and until cars, trains and aeroplanes changed our lives, either riding or being pulled by horses was the quickest way to travel. If you were fighting in wars it was very important to have a good, well-trained horse. He had to be fast and obedient. If your horse was quicker and more obedient than your enemy's, you had a better chance of staying alive. In between wars a lot of time was spent training horses, and sports were invented that tested them, like racing and jousting.

When wars became a little more organised the soldiers who rode horses were called the cavalry. Some of their leading soldiers, that is, their officers, really knew how to train horses well and they became important instructors who handed on their knowledge. The French were especially skilled at this and their word for training horses began to be used in all languages. The word is 'dressage'. It may sound a bit boring, and I think a lot of riders think it is something very special and rather hard to understand. But it is neither of those things, and anyone can learn what it's all about. The difficult part is explaining it to your horse and getting him to co-operate. The important thing to remember is that the word 'dressage' comes from the French *dresser*, which means 'training' and 'deportment'.

The most important word to me is 'deportment' for that means the way a horse carries himself. When we teach our horses dressage we are training them to carry themselves in a well-balanced way. Only when they have learned to do this can they turn, change pace or vary speed with ease. When they can do this they become fun to ride.

Some of you may well be saying: 'But I really just like to jump'! That is good, because you will realise more quickly than anyone else how im-

A well-trained pony is a pleasure to ride.

portant obedience and balance are. Have you ever thought that a show-jumping round is dressage interrupted by fences? In a round of, say, two minutes you might spend seven to nine seconds in the air; the rest of the time is spent getting to the fences and making a good 'get away'. If you arrive at a fence well and leave it well, the jump is bound to be good.

Dressage just means training your horse or pony to be balanced and obedient. But he will also be much happier, because he will understand what you want him to do without your having to pull at his mouth, kick him, or hit him. That's better for both of you.

Nowadays, instead of testing horses in wars we have competitions for them and for ourselves with classes relating to the various stages of training. The most obedient horse usually wins.

But it is not just obedience that counts. It is also the way in which the horse moves. Dressage training should improve your horse's walk, trot and canter, and he will become more beautiful because, like anyone else who takes the right sort of exercise, he will develop good muscles.

A properly trained horse will develop a beautifully arched neck, a strong back, and muscles that hold the saddle in the right place without it slipping forward. His rump will be round and his thighs and hocks will be strong. It is quite possible for horses that have been rather ugly to become beautiful.

There are many reasons for improving the training of your horse or pony by dressage, but the best reason of all is that you yourself will get so much more pleasure out of everyday riding and from the new feeling of understanding that develops between you and your horse.

Of course, you can improve your horse's training without taking part in dressage competitions and can enjoy your riding just as much, but sometimes it can be fun to hear what someone else thinks about your progress. A dressage judge's opinion is especially valuable.

Even if you have only been doing dressage for a short time you will be able to find a competition that is suitable for you. Competitions generally have quite a variety of classes and are graded into different degrees of difficulty, so all the novice horses compete against each other using a simple test that includes nothing more than walk, trot and canter. When you become more experienced and start doing more complicated movements you will compete at a higher standard, and the tests will obviously become more difficult. It's really like school: at the beginning, when you're very young, the things you learn are simple and the exams are easy; as you get older and learn more, the exams get harder until finally they become very difficult indeed.

Making progress from one stage to another happens for two reasons. Firstly, because your horse or pony is learning well, getting

An untrained horse never gives you so much pleasure as a trained one.

stronger and becoming better balanced he will find his work easier. You will then start to do slightly more difficult movements, such as smaller circles and changes from one pace to another exactly where you want to instead of within a few strides. Turns and changes from one direction to another will flow more smoothly and you will be able to halt directly from trot without having to walk first. One day you will discover that the movements you are able to ride belong to a harder level of test. This is the right way to make progress. It is far better than attempting a more difficult test before you are ready.

Secondly, if you have been doing well and winning lots of prizes, you will also have gained 'points'. When you have received a certain number of points you will have to move up to the next standard of test, but until you do so you can compete at the lowest level – and at the higher level, too, if you wish.

Even the best dressage riders in the world take about four years at least before they have trained their horses to the top standard (known as Grand Prix). If you and your horse or pony are learning together it is bound to take longer, and most riders do not achieve the highest level with their first horses. If you have a horse or pony who has ability for dressage and if you yourself really enjoy dressage riding there is no

Every pony or horse can be improved by correct training.

Training means learning good deportment.

reason why you cannot reach the highest national level for 'Ponies' or 'Young Riders'. Certainly the tests ridden at the national championships for your age group should not be too difficult.

Generally speaking it takes a year of training to reach the first standard of walk, trot and canter tests. A year later you might reach the stage when you are showing different kinds of walk, trot and canter

UNTRAINED PONY	TRAINED PONY
Often shows that he doesn't like being ridden – by kicking, napping, rearing or bucking.	*Only does these things when he is overfresh.*
Doesn't respond to a gentle leg aid but needs constant kicks to keep him going.	*Goes forward as soon as he is asked.*
Doesn't stop when a light rein aid is applied but instead leans on your hands and often tries to snatch the reins out of them.	*Is willing and obedient to the rein aids.*
Turns his head very much in one direction, and though he is bent he won't turn or stop.	*Bends slightly in the direction you are travelling in, turns when you ask him to, and stops as soon as you give the correct aids.*
Often has his mouth open.	*Keeps his mouth closed and his jaw relaxed.*
Shakes his head every time you use the reins.	*Keeps his head relatively still.*
Sticks his head in the air and constantly fights you.	*Carries his head in a comfortable position for you both.*
Overbends: that is puts his nose almost on his chest and won't take the contact of the reins.	*Goes forward into the rein.*
When you want to turn, he bends his neck round and looks the way you want to go but keeps moving straight on.	*Turns when you give a small signal.*
On one rein he makes the circle bigger than you want it to be and on the other he cuts in and makes it too small.	*Makes the circles the shape you want them to be.*
Goes faster in trot instead of cantering.	*Strikes off into canter on the aid and without hurrying.*
Breaks into trot when you want to go on cantering.	*Trots only when you tell him to.*
Doesn't go 'on the bit'. (This will be explained later)	*Goes on the bit.*
Won't strike off on the correct leg going in one direction but, instead, always likes to canter with the same leg leading.	*Goes on the correct leg as long as you give the correct aids.*
Jogs when you want to walk.	*Stays in the pace you want to be in.*
Kicks when you tap him with a stick.	*Accepts a tap from your whip and is not afraid of it.*
Seems to have a very bumpy, short stride.	*Develops smooth, comfortable paces.*

A highly trained horse.

(more about these in later chapters). Then a year after that you should be doing 'lateral movements': that is, going sideways and forwards. This stage is known as Medium or M level. It is quite a high standard but you will reach it if you want to!

After that it is very much up to you and your horse.

If you are wondering if it is really worth bothering, just think about the difference between a well-schooled pony and an untrained one.

CHAPTER TWO

How Do You Start?

If you are a member of the Pony Club or of a riding club you probably already know something about dressage. These two organisations run competitions, and each year they hold dressage championships. You will certainly find local dressage competitions in which you will be able to take part.

Generally, clubs not only have competitions but also offer instruction. If you are quite young, the Pony Club is a good organisation in which to begin your dressage riding. If you are not already a member, you will find details of how to join at the back of this book. There is also a list of equestrian organisations in other parts of the world who will tell you about their activities and how to contact local groups.

In Great Britain the British Horse Society (BHS) will help you to find your local Pony Club branch or affiliated riding club. You can also become a junior member of the Dressage Group of the BHS. It is certainly worth considering as they organise training, competitions and talent spotting, as well as being the national body responsible for choosing teams of Pony riders and Young Riders to go to Europe each year to compete against teams from other countries.

As a member you will receive all the latest information on rules and new tests, plus an omnibus schedule with all the official competitions listed in it. Don't let the word 'official' frighten you: there are hundreds of competitions for people just like you, whatever your standard.

In Europe riders in 'Pony Competitions' must ride ponies of 14.2 hands and under and are eligible to compete from the beginning of the year in which they reach the age of twelve until the end of the year in which they reach the age of seventeen.

Riders in 'Young Rider' competitions may ride horses of any size and may take part in competitions from the beginning of the year in which they reach the age of sixteen until the end of the year in which they reach twenty-one.

In Great Britain there are plenty of competitions for ponies and for young riders only, but you are also allowed to ride against adults – and

However experienced you become, you will always need the help of a good instructor.

I have to tell you that adults are often beaten by pony riders!

In some areas the instruction offered by Pony Club branches or riding clubs will be based more on general riding. If you want to specialise you will need to find an instructor who can help you. It is essential to go to someone whom you really like and whom you find easy to understand. You can ask your riding friends if they know of anyone suitable; otherwise you can write to your national equestrian association and ask for advice.

Before you decide to take lessons it is a good idea to watch your chosen instructor at work. You can then get a feeling of whether you would also like to be taught by her or him.

Some adult dressage riders who are not professionals enjoy helping young riders, and you might be lucky and find someone. Never be afraid to ask for help. Most people admire and encourage enthusiasm.

Everyone who trains horses needs help and instruction sometimes, and it is advisable to begin by going to someone knowledgeable. There is nothing worse than discovering that you have been learning all the wrong things.

All through your riding life you will find that instructors offer conflicting opinions, and occasionally you may become rather confused and disheartened. At times like these it is essential to understand that riding a horse is rather different from, say, skiing or riding a bicycle. A horse is a living creature with a mind of his own, so there are many different ways of making him understand what you want. Horses are just like people: they all have different personalities, and need to be approached and communicated with in slightly different ways. It is part of the fun of riding to discover whether your horse needs to be handled firmly or very sympathetically to get the best out of him.

Not only are there many different methods of training a horse, there are also different ways of telling him what to do. It is very important to learn a classical system: one of the four great training methods – German, French, Swedish and Spanish Riding School – which have evolved over hundreds of years. Unfortunately these systems sometimes get a bit muddled up by instructors who have developed their own way of riding. Though muddled systems might work quite well for that particular rider they seldom work for anybody else.

The Spanish and German systems, on which this book is based, are fairly similar and are perhaps the most widely taught and the most successful in international competition. The only real difference between the two is that the Germans tend to ride more strongly, while the Spanish Riding School is softer and gentler: though a great many German riders today are beginning to adopt the softer method, probably because their horses have become lighter and more responsive. (Note that the 'Spanish' system actually stems from the famous Spanish Riding School in Vienna, not from Spain.)

I hope that you are beginning to understand why it is so important to find the right instructor. Unless you learn a clear, logical system you will not only confuse yourself but also your horse.

Unfortunately, although a book can help you a lot it can't teach you about 'feel'. This is the most important lesson to learn when you are training a horse – for unless you can tell from the feeling he gives you that he is going correctly you just won't know.

When you are riding you can only see his head and neck – which is not enough. You have to learn to feel the rhythm, to feel when he is well balanced, when he is correctly on the bit, when he is supple, and most important, when he is going forward correctly. Only an instructor who is watching you can say: 'That's right. Now, can you

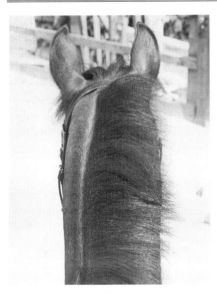

This is the rider's view from the saddle. Unfortunately it often means that he worries only about what the pony's head is doing and completely forgets that the most important part is the hind quarters, which he cannot see.

feel it?' Then you will have to do your best to remember that good feel and recognise it again.

The 'aids' are your signals to your pony. You use your legs against his sides in different places and in different ways; you use your arms and hands through the reins to give gentle signals to his mouth; and you use your back and body to change the feel of your seat in the saddle. When you read about 'the aids' in a book you will probably think to yourself that lots of them sound exactly the same, and you will wonder how your pony will be able to tell the difference. It seems quite a mystery until you realise just how extra-sensitive he is and that he can feel the very slightest difference between one aid and another. Sometimes even you will probably not be able to tell the difference, although your pony knows exactly what to do.

Some riders even refer to the 'thinking' aid – the rider just has to think about the next move and his horse carries it out. What I am pretty sure happens is that when the rider thinks what he wants his horse to do he moves his body very slightly without realising it. The horse senses the smallest movement, even if the rider is unaware of it, and does as he is asked. Very often the smallest possible aid is the best one, for it doesn't disturb the horse's balance.

It is essential for you to learn one specific classical system of aids. You should understand exactly what you must do and when you should do it, and, in between, you must learn to sit quietly. When you really understand exactly *how* you should communicate with your pony you will find that teaching him is relatively easy. But don't

The rider must ask himself, 'Have I been clear?' In this case obviously not because the rider has slipped to the outside of the saddle and is therefore giving confusing aids.

be as stupid as I was when I was about eleven or twelve years old. Let me tell you what I did.

I had a nice pony whom I rode every day. We were really good friends and he generally tried to please me by doing all sorts of things – such as not minding having his feet tied up in hessian sacks so that we wouldn't be heard riding down the road when we went for midnight rides, or swimming in the river. One Christmas I was given a book about how to train a horse properly. I discovered that there were all sorts of things horses were meant to do that I didn't know about, especially something called 'half-pass' which sounded really exciting. I read all about it, and the next day I took my pony out to try. I asked and gave him the right aids - but absolutely nothing happened! I was furious. Why wasn't he paying attention and doing as the book said he should? We nearly stopped being good friends on that day.

It was years later that I realised that my pony should have been given the book for Christmas, too. You see – ponies don't just know the aids. You have to teach them. Some people become angry when their horses don't understand what they want them to do and they even hit the poor creatures in frustration and anger. But just imagine someone coming up to you and speaking in a language you don't understand and then hitting you with a stick because you won't reply. However hard they hit you it would do no good, would it? You still wouldn't understand. When you start getting cross with your pony or horse, just think of *my* stupidity and remember that the mistake is probably yours for not teaching him properly.

Has the pony understood? Apparently not! The rider has asked in the wrong way and now the pony looks very confused.

Just like you, your horse will have to learn your system of aids until the way you speak to him (through the aids) is just as though you were speaking with words in a language which you both understood.

The most important thing is that you learn the language so well that you are always absolutely clear. When you give a signal, say, to canter, you will be sure that you have given it in the correct way and then your horse will learn exactly what you want him to do. With repetition he will become obedient and willing because you are clear in your own mind about how to ask.

Before you get cross with your horse or pony for not being obedient always ask yourself these questions:

1. Have I been clear enough?
2. Has he understood?
3. Can he do what I have asked him to do?

If the answer to any of these questions is 'no', you have no right to be annoyed. In fact, he should be annoyed with you!

You may be a little puzzled by Question 3. But just imagine asking your pony to jump a five-foot wall. He would probably stop, quite simply because he couldn't do it – and you can understand that I am sure. Equally there are movements in dressage that would be just

Good aids are invisible. Flapping legs, like these, are not good aids.

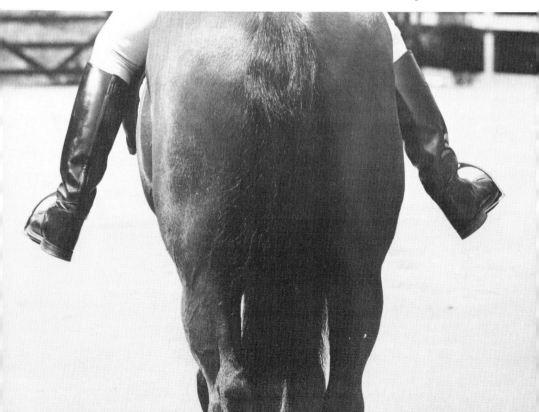

as difficult for a young, untrained horse and therefore impossible, such as very sharp turns or small trot or canter circles. He has to learn with his brain – in other words, to understand – and also with his body. His body has to learn how to do things, too. When you started to ride you probably couldn't trot correctly. Now that you have learned, and your body has become stronger and used to rising up and down, you find it quite easy. In just the same way, your pony's body has to become stronger and more supple.

This is one of the reasons why you will need help from an instructor from time to time. He or she will be able to tell you how to be clear when you give your aids and just how quickly you should expect your horse to learn a new exercise.

Remember, there are bound to be times when his brain will know what you want but his body just won't do what he wants it to do. I sometimes have just the same feeling, don't you?

CHAPTER THREE

Will Any Pony Do?

In the first chapter I explained that dressage training will improve any horse or pony as he becomes more muscled and athletic.

Before a horse has been ridden, and for at least the first three years of his life, he has been free to trot and gallop about, probably playing and even fighting with other young horses. In the same way that small children learn how to walk, then to run and jump, and generally how to manage their bodies efficiently, so young horses develop the same skills.

If you watch a group of two-year-old horses playing together in a field you will see how quick they are at turning, stopping and swerving. Sometimes it's quite frightening to watch them! They pretend to kick at each other; they buck, rear and roll.

Between their third and fourth birthdays they become strong enough to begin the serious training that prepares them for being ridden. Soon they will have to carry a rider on their backs. At first this will feel very strange to them because the new weight on their backs upsets the natural balance which they learned in the earlier years of freedom.

Unfortunately the rider is not able to sit right in the middle of the horse's back where his weight would be distributed equally between his fore and hind legs. There is only one place on which the saddle will stay, and that is just behind the horse's shoulders. Even if a way of keeping the saddle further back was discovered, it would not be a good thing to do because that part of his back wouldn't be strong enough to carry the heavy weight.

So the young horse has to get used to carrying a weight which not only feels too far forward and puts too much weight on his forelegs but which is also moving about all the time and often upsetting his balance even further.

Think of young children of about eighteen months old who have just learned to walk – and how they stagger about and fall over. Watch them try to carry something, and you will see how crookedly it makes them walk. They certainly couldn't possibly carry anything on their backs.

Unlike a child, a foal is able to stand on his feet almost as soon as he is born, partly because he has four legs, but principally because in his wild state a foal is born out of doors where he has to learn to run from danger at his mother's side. As well as giving him the ability to get to his feet within a very short time of being born, nature has also given the horse wonderful strength, stamina and athletic ability. He is fun to ride because he can carry us faster and jump higher than we ever could on our own two legs.

When you start riding a young horse he tires quite quickly, so you stay on his back for just a very short time each day. He therefore has very little time to get used to you before you get off and let him run round in the field on his own again. This is one of the reasons why it takes a young horse so long to find his balance with a rider on his back. If you worked him too hard or for too long it could cause serious damage. His bones are not yet very hard. He has very little muscle and his tendons and ligaments are easily strained.

At first a young horse finds it hard to balance himself.

Month by month you will be able to spend a little more time riding him until, at about the age of four and a half, he can manage an hour or so with a rider in the saddle. By this time he will have become used to carrying a passenger and will feel less unstable. However, unless he has begun proper training with an experienced rider he will still be putting far more weight on his front legs than on his hind legs. This is called 'being on the forehand'.

Only correct training will teach him to put his hind legs further underneath his body and how to bend his hocks and take more weight on them. This gradual alteration of balance from the fore to the hind legs is the basis of dressage training. When a horse has his weight well on his hind legs he will again be able to carry out the gymnastic feats he did when he was running round the fields without a rider. Dressage training means teaching him to carry a rider on his back without losing his balance or spoiling his paces. Remember that it takes a long time for him to change his balance completely, so you have to be patient. Luckily you can feel the change as the months go by and as he develops the extra muscles that he needs to carry you.

Just as some people are better at running and jumping than others, so horses vary. Some are exceptionally skilful at jumping, others excel at galloping, and others are especially good for general riding or dressage.

If your pony has a good temperament and is willing and keen to please, you are lucky. If he is intelligent and learns easily, that is even better. All faults can be improved, if not removed altogether, and that is what training is all about. Obviously it is much easier to teach a willing, energetic horse than a lazy, reluctant one. Horses who shy and are nervous or tense are also difficult, though it is often the rider's fault that they have become like this. Very few horses are really nasty and ungenerous; though unfortunately there are exceptions.

Next to a good temperament, good paces are important. A horse or pony with a good walk, trot and canter has three valuable assets which are more important than appearance. Good looks matter least, for there is no point in having a pretty pony who is so nervous, tense, and anxious that he jogs all the time instead of walking.

It is quite important to understand what good paces are.

The walk should have four regular beats, with each leg spending the same amount of time on the ground and with the same weight put on each leg. A big overtrack – i.e. when the hind foot steps clearly over the print made by the forefoot on the same side – is best. The stride should feel steady and purposeful. There are always at least two legs on the ground at the same time, so there is no feeling of spring in the stride. The walk steps are in this order: right hind, right fore, left hind, left fore. Learn to count and feel the beats when you are riding.

The sequence of walk

Off hind is picked up.

Off fore is picked up.

Near hind is in the air and about to be put down. Near fore is about to be picked up.

Near fore is just being put to the ground as the sequence begins again.

A good forward-going walk.

The trot has two regular beats: first a foreleg on one side and a hind leg on the other side come to the ground together, then the other pair follow suit. These are called diagonal pairs. In between the diagonal pairs of legs touching the ground the horse has all his feet off the ground, which gives the trot a lovely springy feel. This is called the 'moment of suspension'. Again, the steps should be regular and equal and it is also important for the movement to be free and not restricted. Some ponies tend to have rather short, hurried steps. Dressage training can certainly improve this.

FACING PAGE *In trot, first one pair of legs comes to the ground and then, after a moment when all the legs are in the air, the other pair comes to the ground. (*TOP*) The moment of suspension when the near hind and the off fore are about to come to the ground. (*BOTTOM*) The near hind and the off fore are on the ground and after the moment of suspension the off hind and near fore will come to the ground.*

The canter has three beats and then a silent beat when all the feet are off the ground before the next stride begins. First a hind leg comes to the ground, then the diagonal pair, and, finally, the last foreleg (generally called the 'leading' leg), then all the legs are in the air together. A good canter will have a long silent beat; a poor one will have practically none. The canter should be smooth, regular and light, and at the same time energetic and straight.

A horse with good paces will have spring and freedom in his trot and canter and will bend all the joints of his legs so that his action is moderately rounded. In dressage it is not considered ideal for the horse to have a very low action, with his toes passing close to the ground. His legs should not pass too close together at the front or the back, especially when trotting, and the legs should move directly forwards and not swing out or in. In other words he should move with a straight action. Any sign of unlevelness or lameness is considered a severe disadvantage, and although some old ponies with rather stiff joints are still able to be ridden it is not kind to expect them to do gymnastic exercises, which is what dressage really is. Just as elderly humans who are stiff in the joints can manage to walk without too much difficulty, they would not feel so happy going to an aerobics class!

Though the horse's looks don't matter at all as far as the dressage judge is concerned, some points of conformation can cause problems. Although it is probably better not to buy a pony or horse who has such problems, correct training can overcome many of them. There is no such thing as a perfect horse and if you watch top-class dressage you will be surprised by the odd shapes of some of the horses. One of the greatest dressage horses in the world looked really ugly in his stable, yet when he was ridden he looked wonderful. So if your pony has some of the faults mentioned below don't worry or think that there is no point in trying to train him.

The overall picture of the horse is important because he must be in proportion. It is not good, for example, if his shoulders appear strong and big and his hind quarters light.

When he is standing squarely, his hocks should not stick out behind him.

Remember that the hind quarters and the hind legs of the horse are most important, and they must be strong: so a well-rounded rump, a well-developed first and second thigh, and big, strong-looking hocks are what you are looking for. Seen from the side, hind legs which look straight tend to be weak. Seen from behind, the hocks should not point towards each other with the feet outwards.

A hollow or long back is not good. A very short one can also be difficult. The stifle joint should not be much higher than the elbow

Sequence of legs coming to the ground in canter (right canter lead shown).

Near hind (left) comes to the ground first.

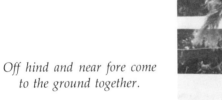

Off hind and near fore come to the ground together.

The leading leg, the off fore (right), comes to the ground, after which there is a moment of suspension when all the legs are off the ground together.

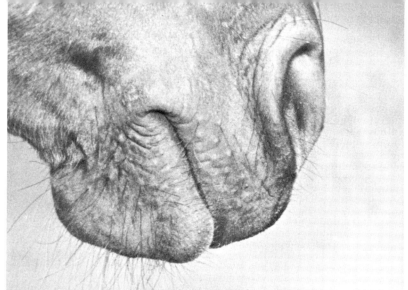

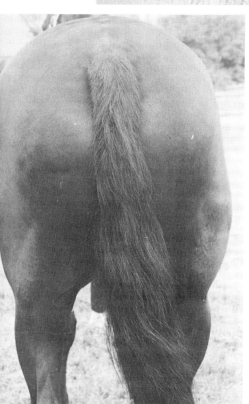

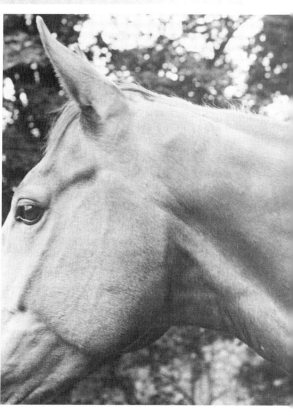

(TOP) *A well-shaped muzzle.* (LEFT) *A good, well-rounded rump with equally well-developed first and second thighs.* (ABOVE RIGHT) *A fine jaw bone with plenty of space behind it.*

of the foreleg. The under-line of the belly should not slope sharply up towards the rear.

The withers should be fairly well pronounced so that the saddle is held in a secure position and does not slip forward towards the shoulder.

The way in which the neck comes out of the shoulder is most important. It should flow out of a sloping shoulder and its top line should have a natural curve. The underside of the neck tells you a great deal about how the horse will carry his head. If there is a big muscle underneath, it is not good. If the muscle just in front of the wither is well developed and the head not carried too low, this is an advantage.

The head should not give the appearance of looking as though it has been stuck on to the neck. If the cheek bone is too big or the neck is too thick at the top there will not be enough space in the gullet to allow correct flexion. Such horses find it difficult to bend at the poll correctly if their cheek bones are sticking into their neck.

A big eye, and a head that seems to be the right size for the body will improve the overall appearance. A narrow mouth and a big tongue can mean that there maybe bitting problems because there just isn't enough room in the mouth for the bit, therefore this causes continual fussing and resistance.

Though it is very easy to dream about the perfect horse, there really is no such thing and most have some faults. The fun is in working together and training your own horse to become more athletic until he overcomes his problems. This is why a good temperament is a very important asset. A willing horse and a keen rider will certainly make the best dressage partnership.

CHAPTER FOUR

Saddles, Bridles and Clothing

A very learned American once said: 'Beware of all enterprises that require new clothes.' What a sensible man he was!

It is quite unnecessary to go out and buy anything new for dressage riding unless the clothes, the saddle and the bridle that you already have are unsuitable because they don't fit. Until you start competing, there are no rules except to remember that it makes sense to wear a correct hat.

The only possible exception might be the bit if it is not one of the permitted snaffles. If you trained your pony in, say, a Pelham, and then when the time came to compete you had to put a snaffle in his mouth, he would almost certainly behave in an unpredictable way.

Let's consider the bridle and the bit first.

THE SNAFFLE BRIDLE

Many different types of snaffle are permitted, and when you get beyond the Novice stage you may use a double bridle. Though there is plenty of choice, the snaffle which you choose for your horse must suit his type of mouth. You will need help in selecting the right one, and even then it is a good idea to borrow before you buy.

Some main types are:

The eggbutt snaffle

This has nice smooth joints where the rings are attached, and a single joint at the centre. The mouthpiece is not especially thick and is therefore suitable for a horse with a rather fat tongue because it does not take up too much room in his mouth. As it is not thick it can be effective if the mouth is rather insensitive.

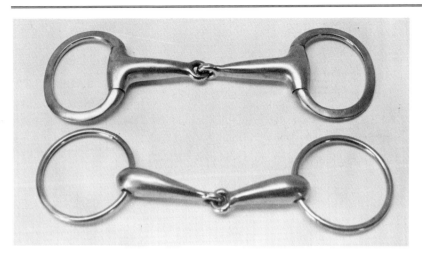

ABOVE: *An eggbutt snaffle (top) and a loose-ringed snaffle.*
BELOW: *A Fulmer with cheek-pieces (top) and a French snaffle with cheek-pieces (bottom).*

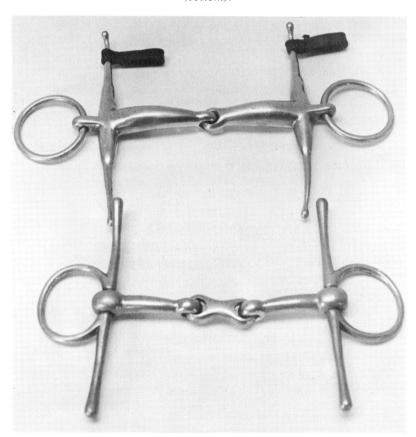

The ordinary snaffle

This has loose rings which are free to turn. Nowadays this bit is often hollow-mouthed and is quite thick and therefore rather comfortable. Because it is hollow it is also quite light, so it doesn't feel heavy in the horse's mouth. It is a good bit if the tongue is not too big. It is light, comfortable and, because the loose rings allow it to be moved, it encourages a wet mouth, which is important.

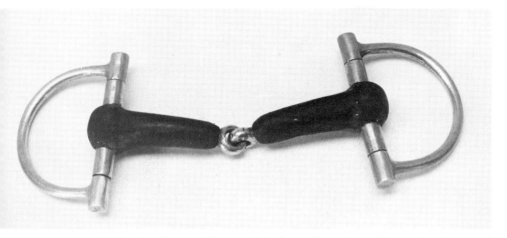

A jointed rubber snaffle – useful when a horse is teething or having mouth problems.

The single-jointed snaffle (sometimes known as a 'Fulmer')

This generally has a thick, heavy mouthpiece. The cheek-pieces are fixed to the sides of the bridle, keeping it very still in the horse's mouth. It can be useful for a horse who fusses and who is unwilling to take a steady contact with the bit. However, some horses tend to lean on it, and it doesn't suit everyone.

The double-jointed snaffle

This can have cheek-pieces, loose rings or eggbutts. It has a flat centre which can be very comfortable for horses with fat tongues because it doesn't pinch the tongue, and the nutcracker action is milder than that of the single-jointed bit. The centre part of the bit must be smooth and must lie flat on the tongue.

Snaffles without any joints can suit some horses (e.g. those with fat tongues). Though they can press down, they don't pinch. Generally they are not used very much.

All these bits can be in metal, rubber, nylon or synthetic material. *Note* The Dr Bristol, which has a centre plate that digs into the horse's tongue, is not allowed in dressage competitions.

Correct fit

One of the most important factors apart from suitability to the shape of your horse's mouth, is width. If the bit is too narrow, it will pinch the corners of the lips. If it is too wide, it will slide sideways through the mouth. The fit should be snug with ¼ – ½ inch to spare at each side when the bit is held straight.

The bit should not be too wide but should fit with about ¼-½ inch free on either side.

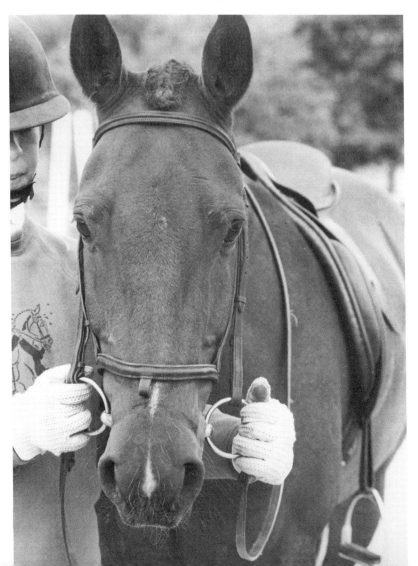

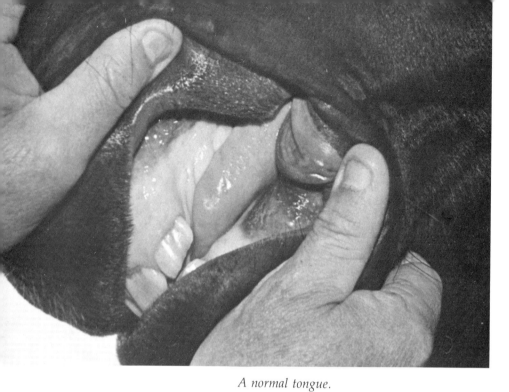

A normal tongue.

A fat tongue, which can lead to bitting problems.

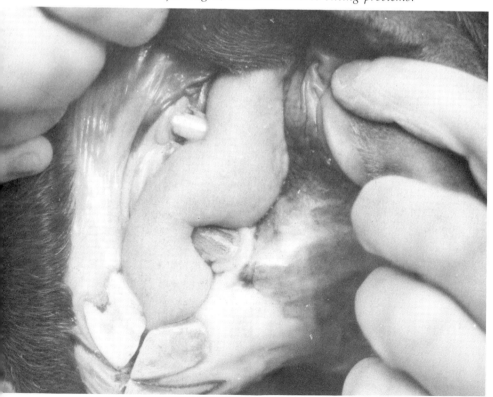

The bridle

Ideally this should be made of leather and should have suitable adjustment in the cheek pieces so that when the bit is fitted the sidepiece buckles come half way down the available holes. The browband should not be too short or it will pull the headpiece forward and pinch the ears. The throatlash must not be too tight because when your horse carries his head correctly the flesh fills up the slack and can prevent him from breathing properly. Many riders like to use either a flash or a drop noseband, which stops the horse opening his mouth and crossing his jaw. If he doesn't try to do this, an ordinary cavesson noseband may be the most comfortable for him.

A well-fitted snaffle bridle with a flash noseband.

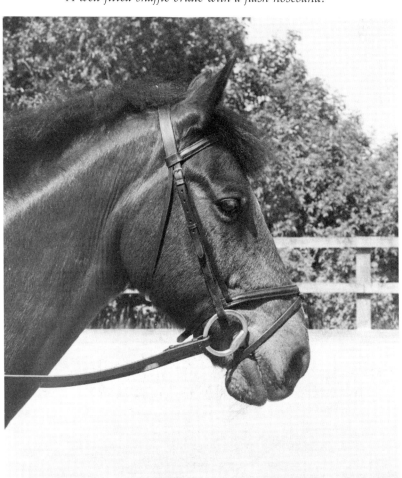

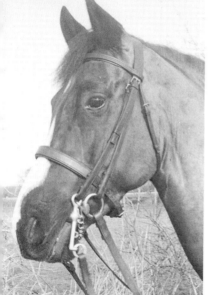

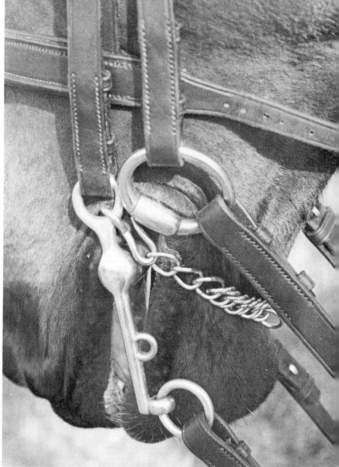

A correctly fitted double bridle and (right) detail of the bits.

I prefer to ride with a rein which is the width of the joint of the fourth finger, nearest the palm. I recommend plain leather reins.

No matter how old, a simple, well-fitting snaffle bridle, when it is well cleaned, is something of which one can be proud.

If it is stiff and dirty – though new and expensive – it is something of which one should be ashamed.

Early training is always carried out in a snaffle, and even when a horse is advanced, much of his training will still be in the snaffle bridle. For the purposes of this book it is enough to say that if your horse will go correctly in a snaffle he will almost certainly confidently accept a double bridle when the time comes. If he will only do dressage in a double bridle there is something wrong with his basic training.

THE SADDLE

One day you will want a special dressage saddle which is designed for riding with long stirrup leathers, but to start with a general purpose saddle that you can also jump in will be much more useful.

There are three main types of saddle:

The dressage saddle

This is cut with straighter flaps, brings your seat bones more forward, and therefore allows your knee to come further under your hip and your leg to stretch down. In this saddle you are able to use your legs to the maximum. The girth straps are very long and a special short girth is used so that the rider doesn't have buckles between his thigh and the horse.

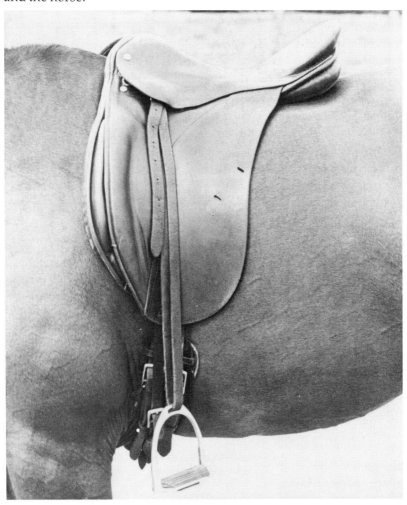

A dressage saddle.

The jumping saddle

This has a very forward-cut flap and a seat which encourages the seat bones to move further back, enabling the stirrups to be shortened and helping the rider to balance more easily, although to some extent he loses the influence of his legs.

The general–purpose saddle

This is a cross between the dressage and the jumping saddle and is therefore a good compromise for the rider who trains his horse correctly on the flat and who also wants to jump.

Saddle fitting

It is essential for the saddle to fit the horse and the rider. If it does not fit the horse it will also be uncomfortable for the rider.

A general-purpose saddle.

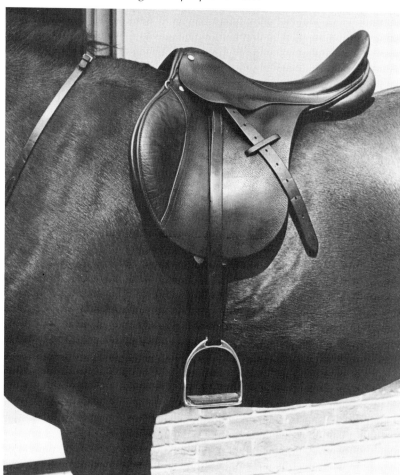

The width of the saddle at the front is critical. If it is too wide, it will press on the withers and give the horse a sore back. If it is too narrow, it will pinch and be so high in front that the rider's seat will slide to the back of the saddle and he will not be able to prevent his legs from sticking forward. He will find it hard to balance.

When the width is correct the bearing surface should be spread well over the horse's back so that the rider's weight is well distributed. A small bearing surface often results in a sore back. Unfortunately some modern saddles have a small bearing surface.

The seat of the saddle should not 'grip' the rider, but should allow him to move. If the lowest part of the saddle is well forward, he will be helped to sit in the correct position; but he must not feel trapped.

The stirrup leathers should not be bulky under the leg, and the stirrups should be large enough to give half an inch extra space beside the boot. If there is too much space there could be a danger of the foot sliding through and becoming trapped.

General notes on tack

Martingales are not allowed in dressage competitions and are seldom used in training. Breast plates and neck straps *are* permitted.

While training, it is sensible to protect your horse's legs with bandages or boots, but these are *not* allowed in competition.

Protective boots should be used during training.

Generally speaking, bright-coloured girths, saddles, reins or other equipment should be avoided. There is no substitute for the lasting quality and the looks of real leather, whatever its age.

CLOTHES FOR THE RIDER

Young dressage riders may wear jodhpurs and jodhpur boots. Ideally the jodhpurs should be beige and the jodhpur boots brown.

For more senior riders, black or brown hunting boots with white, cream or beige breeches are correct.

A white or cream shirt with a collar and tie or a coloured stock look well under a tweed coat and are correct for the younger age group. A hard cap, with or without a chin strap, or a bowler hat, must be worn. Navy blue or black are the most favoured colours.

A correctly dressed young competitor. A chin strap is recommended.

An impeccably dressed young rider competing at advanced levels.

Senior riders generally prefer a black or navy coat, which should be worn with a white or cream stock rather than a coloured one. It is, however, quite correct to ride in a tweed coat right up to Advanced standard. At Advanced level, a top hat and tail coat are generally worn.

Gloves must be worn, and the backs must be of a light colour.

Tidiness and cleanliness are important. Unless you have plaits, a pony tail, or very short hair, you should wear a hair net.

Well-polished boots, a well-brushed and pressed jacket, and spotless breeches really look good and are worth the effort. Fasten down your stock or tie so that it won't flap about.

Wearing more than one badge on your lapel looks rather messy; if you do wear a badge, make sure that it is polished.

In competitions you will probably have to wear a number. Make sure that it is firmly attached or tied and that the ends are tucked through your waist buttonhole so they don't fly about.

In Novice and Elementary tests you are allowed to wear spurs. In Medium and above, they *must* be worn. They should be made of metal and correctly fitted. Rules vary a little, so read the relevant book before competing. Whips can generally be carried: but, again, rules vary so it is better to check.

Of course, the above-mentioned clothes are all for competitions. When you are training you can wear whatever you like, though it is sensible to wear proper breeches, boots, hat and gloves so that you will not feel unnatural when dressed for competitions.

When you are training, you should always carry a schooling whip – not for punishment, but to back up your leg aids. Your horse should not be afraid of the whip, so the best way to make him confident is always to carry one and never misuse it.

When you are training at home, wear clean, workmanlike clothes. Your horse should feel proud to have you on his back. An untidy appearance implies a rather untidy mind, and you need a very tidy mind to train a horse well.

CHAPTER FIVE

The Rider and His Position

As you have already learned, the young horse has difficulty in getting used to carrying a rider on his back. When the rider moves about in the saddle it is even more difficult for the horse to find his balance. If the weight in the saddle is constantly changing its position, the horse has to keep changing the way in which he carries himself.

The best riders help their horses to maintain balance by not bumping about, changing positions or losing their own balance. They make the burden of carrying a passenger as easy as possible by letting their body flow with the movements of the horse. This is the secret of good dressage riding.

I'm sure that you have often given a piggy-back to a friend or small sister or brother. The 'riders' who do not move or stiffen are much easier to carry than those who throw their weight about or who are frightened and tense. Imagine yourself trying to cross a narrow bridge carrying someone on your back who is always moving from one side to the other. This is just how the young horse feels when he is trying to go in a straight line and his rider keeps moving and making him lurch from side to side.

Learning to ride well means learning to sit on your horse in a balanced way that makes you the easiest possible burden to carry.

When you first ride, your natural instinct is to hang on and lean forwards. Gradually, as you gain more confidence, you start to sit up and relax. Most riders have quite good balance at the walk and are able to sit in a way that makes their weight easy to carry. In trot the movement of the horse is far more energetic and the rider is thrown about, bumping in the saddle.

The rider soon learns the rising trot and finds it a great relief, while sitting trot remains a problem. Canter is much faster and the horse moves with even more energy. The beginner, who finds the pace quite alarming at first, bumps up and down, leans forward, stiffens and clutches the horse's sides with his legs. The horse generally goes faster, the rider is frightened, and everything becomes worse.

Learning to ride well means learning to keep your balance and to harmonise with the movement of the horse at all paces. This is why the correct position matters; it is not just because it looks pretty. When the rider is balanced and in harmony he can sit softly and quietly and is then able to give signals to his horse.

Imagine being a horse carrying someone who is bumping in the saddle, jerking the reins and kicking with his legs by mistake. The horse is a kind and tolerant animal, so he gets used to all the strange bumps and jerks, but how can he be expected to tell the difference between these movements and the rider's intended signals for stop, start, turn or change pace? Of course, he can't. He has learned to ignore them. Yet sometimes a rider will say: 'My horse isn't concentrating; he won't listen to me.'

Are you beginning to feel sorry for the horse? Good! That means you understand why it is important to ride well and to improve *yourself* before you try to improve your horse. The rider who wonders what he has done wrong when his horse won't do something is the rider who will train his horse best. The rider who always blames the horse is seldom right.

Finding perfect balance on a horse is not easy – for, unlike a bicycle, a horse tends to do rather surprising things. It is only when you become confident, your muscles become trained, and your reactions become sensitive and quick that you can begin to overcome your natural reactions to hang on at all costs.

Unfortunately, when you ride, you have very little time to concentrate fully on your own position because most of your thoughts are taken up with thinking about the horse and getting him to go in the right direction and at the right pace.

This is why riding on the lunge, with someone else in charge of the horse, is so valuable. A lunge lesson is a riding lesson for you and you only. You can concentrate on those parts of your body that behave badly and you can even start to think about those parts that are doing the right thing.

The riding teacher who makes a lunge lesson a painful business is not doing a very good job. He should be making you feel comfortable and at ease on your horse. He should be helping you to discover the feel of riding correctly. Once your body discovers that it is easier to do something correctly it will quickly give up its bad habits.

In most countries whose riders excel at dressage, young riders learn to ride on the lunge. They therefore begin with a great advantage.

Unfortunately if you have learned to stay on a horse without having proper instructions in the beginning you will probably have used all sorts of muscles to keep you in the saddle. What you should have learned is the correct position from which you can balance yourself without effort.

A good rider doesn't tire himself greatly. A bad one feels very well exercised when he gets off. He has been using all his muscles to stay on board.

You will certainly need experienced help with your position. The younger you are, the better: for young bodies are supple and elastic and, just like the young horse, are ready to learn and develop new skills.

However, certain basics can be learned from a book. Certainly, how your body should look and feel while riding is one of them.

THE POSITION AT THE HALT

You have two bones in your seat which support you in the saddle. While you are reading this, see if you can feel them. Sit on a hard chair with both hands underneath you. I'm sure you will discover your seat bones! It is very important to feel these two bones when you are sitting in the saddle, because you must learn to balance on them when you are riding – exactly as you do on your two legs when you are walking. Remember that learning to walk took you quite a long time when you were very small.

Think of the two bones as being like the rockers on an old-fashioned rocking horse. You can swing backwards and forwards on them, but at rest you will always come back to the centre and be still. Finding the centre is important. Everyone has his or her own centre. Find it like this:

When you are sitting on your horse lift your knees up very high (like a jockey) and sit up as straight as you can. Get someone to check that your shoulders are directly above your hips. Now feel your seat bones. Slowly, lower your legs and take up your stirrups without changing the feel or the position of the seat bones. Now you have found their centre. Remember this feel, and always return to it: it is your correct upright position. Your shoulder will be above your hip and your heel directly under your hip, so a straight line could run through them and meet the ground at right angles. If you lean forwards or backwards even slightly you will find that you have to grip a little with your legs to stop yourself falling forwards or backwards. In other words, you have lost your balance. Correct balance on your seat bones is the key to successful dressage riding.

From this position it is easy to let the thigh lie softly against the saddle with the lower leg resting against the horse's side, the toe pointing almost directly forwards and the heel a little lower than the toe. The stirrup should take the weight of the foot, with the ball of the foot on the bar of the stirrup.

The rider should sit in an upright but natural way. His shoulders should not be forced back but he should feel as though he is growing upwards while his shoulders remain 'heavy' and growing downwards. His head should not stick forward but should remain perfectly upright.

The reins should be held between the fourth finger and the little finger, with the fourth finger closed securely around the rein. There should be a line from the rider's elbow down the forearm and the back of the hand, and down the rein to the horse's mouth. Wherever the horse puts his head, that line should remain the same. The elbows should always be in front of the rider's body. The rider moves his arms at the elbow and the shoulder joint when he follows the to and fro movement of the horse's head. If only one of these joints is moved, the line to the horse's mouth will be broken.

There will be a lot more about the rider's hands and arms in further chapters. The feel of the rein in the rider's hands is called 'the contract' and I will be explaining about it quite a lot later on.

THE POSITION OF THE RIDER AT WALK, TROT AND CANTER

When the horse moves, the rider moves, too. If he didn't, both he and his horse would feel very uncomfortable.

There are two kinds of movement that the rider makes: those that

The correct position at the walk.

are in harmony with the horse and those that give a signal to the horse.

It is often said that a really good rider 'looks part of the horse'. What this really means is that the rider has learned to move *with* the horse instead of just sitting on it as best he can.

To move with the horse you have to move your hip joints and your back.

While you are sitting still and upright, push your tummy forward and feel how your hips and back move. This is the movement that you make when you are riding.

In walk, with each sequence of the horse's steps the rider's tummy will push forward and then relax (allowing the tummy, hips and spine to return to the upright position). The rider makes his tummy go forward and – just as when you lift your arm and then lower it – it is the forward movement that needs the effort. The return, or the lowering, is just controlling the body's return to normal. Lift your arm and lower it and you will see which requires most effort!

In rising trot, the rider is changing from sitting on his seat bones to balancing on his feet. It is as simple as that: rather like getting up out of a chair. You lean a little forwards until your hips are balanced over your feet. Returning to the saddle is the same. You steadily transfer

This young rider is nicely balanced as she rises to the trot.

ABOVE: *This is the sitting moment of the rising trot.*

BELOW: *A good position in sitting trot demonstrated by one of the best riders in the world, Dr Reiner Klimke.*

ABOVE: *A good position at canter.*
BELOW: *The same rider and the same moment in the canter, but here she is leaning too far forward.*

your weight from your feet to your seat bones. The danger comes in doing this too suddenly, because you are not careful enough when you transfer your balance from your feet to your seat. The poor horse often gets a nasty bang in his back as a result. Try to think of the horse's back and how he feels if you keep on flopping into the saddle.

Sitting trot is just like a walk except that it happens far more quickly. The rider must swing his tummy forward much more quickly, which at first is rather difficult.

In order to make sitting trot more comfortable, some riders either lean backwards or they round their back. This collapsing or rounding of the back on every stride is both common and comfortable, but it prevents you from using your back correctly to encourage impulsion and rhythm.

In canter, because the horse swings to and fro with a rocking action, the rider's body also must feel as though it is swinging backwards and forwards. What really happens is that the rider's seat stays in the saddle while his shoulders stay still. This feels to the rider as though he is leaning backwards and forwards, though of course all he is doing is staying upright. There is also the same feeling of the tummy pushing forwards.

Bouncing in the saddle in canter is common. It happens when a rider stiffens his hips as he feels his shoulders moving back. A feeling of riding a rocking horse or sitting on a swing will help to develop a smooth canter position.

In all movements except rising trot, the rider's seat should stay close to the saddle.

The most important thing is to be so balanced that you won't have to tighten unnecessary muscles, and then to let your back and hips absorb the movements of the horse.

Only from this position will you be able to apply correct aids and not hinder your horse.

NOTE* The author's book *Balanced Riding*, also published by Threshold Books, deals with the position of the rider in great depth.

CHAPTER SIX

Talking to Your Horse

Though horses don't use words to communicate with each other, they have a body language that is just as efficient. If we are to understand them and to learn how to train them we have to employ a body language of our own which they can understand.

Though horses respond to our voices, it is generally to the tone rather than to the actual words. 'Good' is usually said in a soothing, pleasant way. 'Steady' is even more drawn out and calming. Calling them in from the field is always done in a certain type of voice that they recognise. 'Trot' or 'Trot on' are usually rather brisk and sharp. When your horse is cantering, on the lunge for example, and you want him to return to trot, you use quite a different tone and your voice goes from a high note to a low one –'Ter-rot'.

Without realising it, you are speaking in a language which the horse can understand. You may think that it is the words they have learned but really it is the tone and the inflection of your voice. Try another word of the same length and with the same amount of syllables, and say it in the same way as your normal word – 'Bad', for example, instead of 'Good' – and you will find that it works just as well!

Horses love to be spoken to gently and soothingly, and they certainly respond to encouragement. It is very important to develop *your* way of talking to *your* horse. When you are riding, watch his ears when you say 'good boy'. You will find that he is really listening to you.

Horses are equally sensitive to touch. Watch two of them in a field nibbling each other's necks just in front of the withers. This is a very sensitive area, and they really enjoy this mutual 'back-scratching'. Try scratching your horse in this particular place. If you are standing with his head over your shoulder he may start nibbling your back, too! When you are with him in the stable try to discover places where he likes being scratched or stroked. Learning to communicate in this way will help you form a real friendship with him. It is very important, for he must love you and want to please you.

When you are riding and he does something well, a little rub with your fingers just in front of his withers will tell him that you are pleased, and it will make him happy, too.

So far we have just thought about voice and touch, which we also use for communicating with other human beings.

Now we have to think about much more complicated ways of telling our horses what we want them to do. Luckily they are very responsive to feel. Far more, in fact, than we are, for we tend to respond to words more than anything else.

There are two very important things to learn. Firstly, through feeling what is happening underneath you, you must learn to understand what your horse is telling you. Secondly, you must learn through your body to tell your horse what you want him to do.

This body language has to be like a conversation – with both of you sometimes listening and sometimes speaking. It has to be a two-way communication.

The signals which you give to your horse are called the 'aids'. It is rather unfortunate that there is not a special word in our equestrian language for the way in which the horse speaks back to us, but in this book I am going to call it 'response'.

Remember that your horse will tell you everything you need to know without words, but you have to be listening to *his* language. You don't listen with your ears: you listen with your body, and that is called 'feel'.

Unless you develop your ability to feel you will never be a dressage rider – or a rider of any sort for that matter.

By using your back, seat, legs and hands you are able to give small signals to the horse which, after training, become the language which you transmit to him. He will learn this language in almost the same way that you might learn a foreign language at school, little by little. If you are not clear in the way in which you teach him this new language he cannot possibly be expected to understand or to respond obediently. He may do his best to please you, and may try guessing at what you have asked him to do, but it will probably be a bad guess. The result will be that he worries and becomes upset. You may think that he is being disobedient.

As I have already explained in an earlier chapter, it is very important for you to learn a classical system of aids (the language of signals).

The terms 'inside' and 'outside' leg are often used when referring to the legs and hands. The inside leg is always the leg that is on the inside of a circle or turn. So if you are circling to the right, the inside will be the right leg or hand and the outside will be the left leg or hand. You will have to become familiar with these expressions because they are a very important part of the horseman's language.

The 'bend' of the horse is another important word. When a horse moves on a circle to the right he must curve his body a little in that direction. If, instead, he turns to the outside he is said to be 'incorrectly bent'. Counter canter, explained on page 121, is the only exception to these two rules.

THE LEG AIDS

The legs create impulsion (which is energy *not speed*). They also control the quarters.

The leg aid, if applied just a little behind the girth – without moving backwards or forwards from its normal position – sends the horse forward or asks for more energy. The inside leg also asks for the correct bend. The leg can be applied with an inward nudge or pressure. As the training of the horse progresses, the leg aid must become almost invisible. The rider's toes should remain pointing forwards and his

(LEFT) The inside leg on the girth creates impulsion and bend and (RIGHT) the outside leg behind the girth controls the quarters.

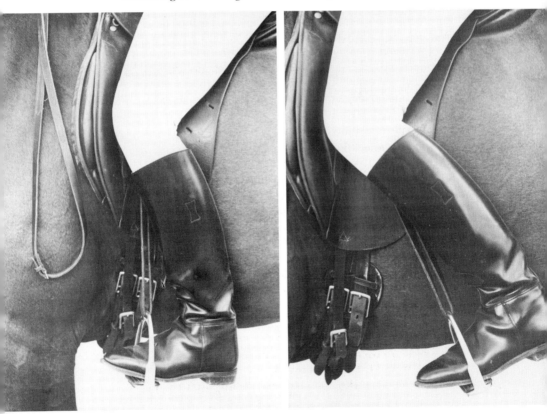

legs should never be lifted away from the horse's sides before the aid is given.

Applied further behind the girth, the leg can either support, by stopping the quarters swinging that way, or ask for the hind leg on the side where it is applied to move forwards and sideways away from the leg that is giving the aid.

If the rider's thigh and seat muscles are tense and his knee is gripping he will find it almost impossible to give quick, light leg aids. His lower leg will have been forced away from the horse's side.

THE REIN AIDS

The outside rein supports and controls the speed; the inside rein asks for direction and bend.

Used together with the body and legs the reins are used to:

Change from a faster pace to a slower one (make transitions).
Slow down within the pace (shorten the stride).
Bend or flex the horse.
Halt and rein back.

The rein aids should never be applied with a backwards pull but just a squeeze of the fourth finger. The rein aid must always be applied briefly. Any pulling backwards or prolonged pulling on the reins is incorrect. A steady contact of the reins should always be kept with a very brief increase followed by an instant decrease or yielding of the rein.

Rein aids must never be applied on their own but always with body and legs.

The hands must be carried with the thumbs uppermost and the hands equally positioned on either side of the withers. Remember that the line elbow-hand-horse's mouth must be kept so that the height of the hands will depend on the posture of the horse. A young horse begins by carrying his head rather low, but as training progresses and his balance moves further towards the quarters, he will carry his head higher.

The rider's hands should never cross the withers.

THE BODY OR WEIGHT AIDS

The body or weight aids are the ones which influence the horse most. They are also the most invisible, so it is difficult for an instructor to know whether you are carrying them out correctly.

The rider influences the horse with his body by:

Putting his weight on both seat bones.
Putting his weight on one seat bone.
Taking his weight off both seat bones.

The horse will feel the influence of the rider's seat on every stride. If the rider moves his back and hips correctly and remains in balance he will be able to influence and regulate the rhythm of the horse's stride, create more energy and develop collection.

Just as you can't make a good cake with only flour or sugar or eggs but can make a very good one by mixing them all together in the right quantities, so you will learn that one aid on its own will not produce very much effect and you must find the right 'mixture' or co-ordination of your signals. One aid is nearly always dependent on another, and certainly the rein aids should never be applied without the support of legs or body weight.

The leg and body aids are the most important. In a well-trained horse the rein aids are the least used.

In these last two chapters I have given some simple outlines about how you should sit and how you should give signals to your horse.

Throughout your riding life I hope you will always try to think about improving your position and the way in which you communicate with your horse. Riders generally only improve or get worse; they never stay the same. Always remember the important question when something goes wrong: Is it my fault?

CHAPTER SEVEN

Obedience

Until your horse understands some of the very basic aids you will not be able to help him improve his balance or his paces.

The first lesson he must learn, whatever his age, is to go forward willingly. Until he learns that a little nudge with your leg means that he must respond by increasing his energy, further training will be impossible.

For this reason you should always carry a schooling whip, which

The way to use the schooling whip.

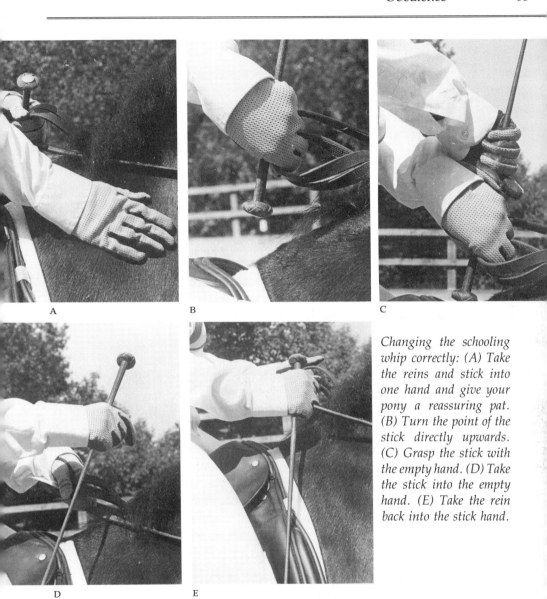

A   B   C

D   E

Changing the schooling whip correctly: (A) Take the reins and stick into one hand and give your pony a reassuring pat. (B) Turn the point of the stick directly upwards. (C) Grasp the stick with the empty hand. (D) Take the stick into the empty hand. (E) Take the rein back into the stick hand.

is a long, light whip that you can use just behind your leg without taking your hand off the reins. Preferably it should be carried in your inside hand, so whenever you change direction (change the rein) you must also change the hand in which you carry the whip. The reason is simple. The whip is used to correct your horse's disobedience to your leg. Your inside leg is the one that you will use to create more impulsion, so this is the side on which the whip should be used.

Your horse should not be afraid of the whip, and he must be confident when you change it from one side to another.

To change from the right hand to the left, first put both reins into the whip hand and pat his neck with the left hand. Now turn the hand with the reins and whip so that the little finger side is uppermost (instead of the thumb side).

Take the whip with the left hand by grasping it thumb side down. Let go of the whip with the right hand and take the reins back into each hand. It sounds rather complicated and at first it is a little difficult, but with practice you will soon find it by far the easiest way, and the least upsetting to your horse. If he is nervous of the whip because he has been upset by it in the past you must retrain him. Start with a very short stick and gradually use a longer and longer one.

Never misuse the whip by using it repeatedly. A tap is usually enough, but if your horse is very lazy and disobedient he may need quite a sharp tap to teach him to go forward. If he responds by *jumping* forward, even into canter, allow him to do so for a few strides and pat him before you quietly bring him back to the pace you require. After all, you asked him to go forward. The fact that he has overreacted is good – but next time remember to tap more gently.

You often see a rider hitting his horse when he won't go forward – and then immediately pulling on the reins when he does. I'm sure you can understand that this is very confusing for the horse. Soon he will think that his rider wants him to do nothing when he is hit, and the rider will try hitting him even harder!

When you use the whip, be careful never to do so in anger. If you find that you have gritted your teeth, you may be using your whip for the wrong reasons. It is easy to feel angry with yourself then blame the horse instead.

While you are teaching your horse to go forward, try to keep a light but even contact of the reins. Though he should feel the contact of the reins on the bit it must not be uncomfortable or it will stop him moving forward in a natural way. Don't worry at this stage about his being 'on the bit'.

Teaching him to go forwards with obedience is best in rising trot. Your aim is to feel him swinging along with a nice active trot that is energetic and regular. Rhythm is very important, and you should try to keep the trot as regular as possible, though at this stage it can be quite difficult.

Your voice plays an important part in this early training, and a cheerful encouraging tone will help him along.

Your own position in rising trot is very important. You must be very well balanced, so that you are able to bring your seat back into the saddle on each stride without banging your horse's back. This is

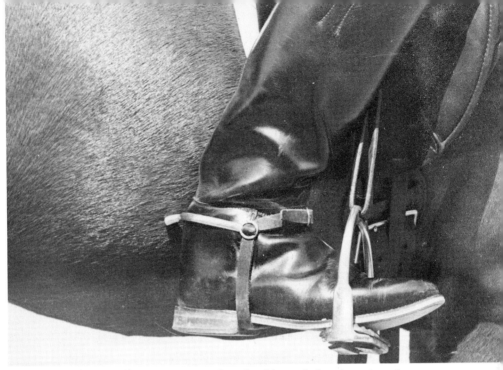

Correctly used spurs. If spurs are worn they should merely brush against the horse's sides.

Incorrectly used spurs. If the toes are turned out, the end of the spurs will dig into the horse's sides.

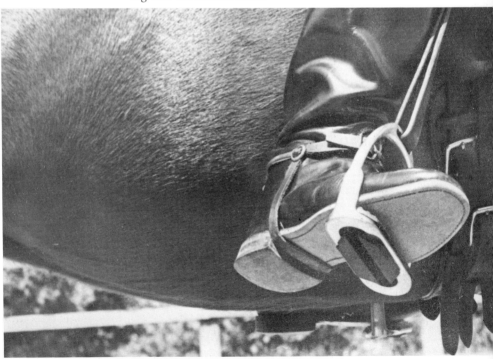

especially important with a young horse. Sometimes with an older one, whose back is well muscled, a little stronger use of the weight as it returns to the saddle can produce more impulsion.

Remember: if your horse is young, do give him plenty of walking periods, and don't make your lessons very long.

If he is an older horse who is lazy and unresponsive, too much work in the school will not be a good idea, as he will become bored. Learning to go forward may be accomplished more quickly if you can take him on cross-country rides with another free-going horse.

It should not take more than a few days to make your horse understand that he must go forward when asked – but he will never learn if you constantly kick his sides with your legs and repeat aids to which he has already responded. Only if you learn to sit still after he has responded to leg or whip will he realise that this is what you want. He will learn even more quickly if you praise him with a caress or with your voice.

When your horse is going well it is all very easy to keep him going and to try to make him go better still: but this is greedy and rather stupid. Think of it from his point of view. He has already done as you have asked, and now you are asking for something else. Perhaps what he has already done was not correct. Perhaps he should try something different in order to please you.

When your horse gives you something that you have asked for by responding correctly to an aid, it is very important for you to tell him so in one way or another. He will appreciate praise, a caress, a titbit, or, above all all, rest.

You cannot expect your horse to respond to rein aids until he is going forward correctly. This will not happen until he is using his quarters energetically, with that energy bringing his hind legs forward under him and going right through his body so that finally you feel it coming back to you through the reins.

The 'swinging' feel is essential. The horse generally starts off each training session by tightening his back and neck muscles as he feels the weight of the rider. Gradually, as you work in trot with simple exercises, these muscles loosen and he lets the energy flow through his body. You will learn to recognise the feeling and know that you must not ask anything further of the horse until he gives it to you.

Remember: 'forward' does not mean 'faster'. It means working with energy.

Some of you will have horses who have too much energy and like to go too fast. Generally they are tense and nervous. They tend to jump when you use your legs and are often frightened of the whip. Though it feels as if they have too much impulsion, they are using their energy just to make their legs go faster. These horses must also learn to use their back and neck muscles and to trot with true impulsion and swing. Because they are just using their legs they will often lose their balance and their rhythm. They will certainly not be able to respond to correct rein aids.

Again, it is essential for such horses to learn to work through their bodies before you can do anything else.

One of the most difficult lessons to teach a horse is that the leg aid does not mean faster, only 'more energy'. In order to achieve this, a soft, steady rein contact is essential. When you ask him to go forward you are therefore riding him towards the rein contact. Your hand must never pull backwards.

With a young horse especially, but also with a horse who is unresponsive to your rein aids, your voice will be a great help in teaching downward transitions and halt aids.

He should have learned in his early training on the lunge to respond to voice commands. If he has forgotten these it is quite easy to re-train him.

Always use the same tones when you speak to him, and for downward transitions make sure that your voice is calming.

To walk from trot: **Wa-alk** (said in a drawn-out way on two notes, high to low).

To stop: **Whoa** (a steady single note, slightly drawn out, never sharp).

In Europe young horses are trained to stop when they hear 'Brrrrrr!' This is very effective, though not heard much in Great Britain.

Your horse will soon respond to your voice and then you can add the rein aids at the same time.

To make a downward transition, squeeze the ring or fourth finger of the outside rein and as soon as you feel a response, stop squeezing.

Until your horse understands this very simple language of the legs and the reins you will not be able to improve his paces or his balance. They are the stepping stones to progress.

During this early schooling work, and once your horse is going forward willingly, repeated walk-trot transitions will be helpful in developing obedience and response. Use your voice and whip to help you. Never start thumping with your legs or pulling on the reins.

Always reward obedience and soon you will find that you have a willing, responsive horse instead of a confused, unwilling or anxious one.

Patience and time at this stage will be rewarded and later on you will realise how very important these early lessons have been.

Sometimes I will refer to 'the school'. By this I do not necessarily mean an elaborate manège, but rather the place where you work your horse. This should be a flat area of at least 20 metres × 40 metres. If you have a large, flat field you are very lucky. Later on you will have to mark out a dressage arena, for which you will only need twelve cans! Of course, boards look smarter but they are not really necessary.

CHAPTER EIGHT

Rhythm and Tempo

When we refer to the rhythm we mean the regularity and evenness of the steps. In trot, a regular rhythm is when the sound of the hoof-beats stays at exactly the same speed and does not vary by quickening or slowing down.

Tempo means the speed of the hoof-beats – that is, the time. It can be quick or slow. A horse can trot quickly or slowly without losing rhythm.

Until a young or untrained horse has improved his balance it is quite difficult to decide what is his correct tempo. It presents a problem, because every horse has a speed that suits him and is natural to the way in which he is made. The length of his legs and his ability to spring and move freely will all affect the tempo which is correct for him.

It is more dangerous to go too fast than too slowly. Generally speaking, the horse who hurries and goes with quick, rather short steps is only using his legs instead of his whole body.

Humans often do this too. Think of how a really good athlete, such as a tennis player or runner, uses his whole body. Compare him with someone who seldom runs, or maybe with a woman in high heels; they tend to hold their bodies quite still, with their arms close to their sides, and jog along with short steps. The difference is very clear and the variation in the speed at which they travel is even more obvious.

For horses to make the best use of their wonderful ability they, too, must use their whole bodies – and short, hurried steps will not encourage this.

In trot, some horses take very long, springy strides, and although this looks beautiful it is sometimes necessary to ride them in a slightly quicker tempo to make them use their bodies and engage their hind legs. This type of horse can be very difficult to collect.

It is really a question of finding out what is correct for your horse. However, you cannot establish the ideal trot tempo until your horse is going forward properly into the reins. If he is lazy and unwilling, it may be best to quicken his tempo a little to teach him to be energetic. If he is nervous and hurries anxiously, you may have to slow him down considerably so that he is forced to use his body to balance himself. Only when he starts using his body can you add more impulsion.

Let us think again about trot, for this is the pace in which you will work most for the time being. In an earlier chapter you learned that the trot has two distinct beats as the diagonal pairs of legs (front leg on one side and back leg on the other) come to the ground. In between each pair of legs touching the ground there is a moment called the 'moment of suspension', when all the legs are off the ground together. This moment in the air is very important. If your horse has a tempo that is too quick he will spend almost no time at all in the air because his next pair of feet are busy getting to the ground. If he is very lazy and goes without impulsion he will practically step from one set of legs to the other without springing at all. This is the type of trot that the dressage judge calls 'earthbound'. Then there is the horse with so much spring that he spends too long in the air!

Whatever length of stride you ask your horse to take, the tempo and the rhythm should be the same. Here the strides are long.

Here the same horse is taking shorter strides.

As a rider you have to decide what your horse's problem is and experiment a little with various tempos.

Generally speaking, by slowing down the speed yet keeping the energy and the feel of 'forward' your horse will be forced to stop catching himself with another short step; instead he will learn to move his weight on to his hind legs a little more. When the hoof-beats sound slower there will be time for him to take longer strides and spring a little more into the air. In other words, the moment of suspension will become longer. But do remember that it is no good just slowing down. You have to encourage him to be energetic, too.

It is only when he starts engaging his hind quarters a little more and springing along with better strides that a really good rhythm can develop.

Until your horse is really using his whole body without tension or tightening his back and neck muscles he cannot possibly be supple. If his muscles are tense through nervousness or lack of correct working-in you will not be able to establish a good swinging rhythm.

Finding real rhythm is a lovely feeling for both you and your horse. When the back and neck muscles lose their tension, your horse is able to use his whole body in conjunction with his legs. All joints must bend and stretch.

True regularity is only developed through having a mixture of suppleness, looseness and activity. When you achieve it you will feel as though you and your horse are dancing to music. Together you will feel and move in perfect rhythm. This is sometimes called 'cadence'.

Your horse will enjoy this way of going and you will see that his ears are pricked and that he works calmly without being distracted. If you listen to his breathing you will hear a regular blow with each stride, which shows how well harmonised his whole body is and how natural this work is for him. If you were watching him you would see his tail swinging like a pendulum, to and fro. After the trot work is established you will be able to discover the same feeling in canter and walk. Though the beats are different and though there is no spring in walk, you should feel the same regularity, whether it is three beats or four, and the same forwardness and swing.

The horse's tail will swing like a pendulum, to and fro.

This pony is stretching down and really using his back in walk.

Perhaps it is becoming clearer to you now that speed is not impulsion. In fact sometimes speed stops your horse going with impulsion. Remember, impulsion means moving with energy not with speed. Only energy that involves the whole of the horse's body is true impulsion.

As a rider you can influence your horse a great deal at this stage of his training.

As long as you have established the simple obedience to the leg and rein aids (as explained in the last chapter) you will be able to help your horse to develop this important rhythm and balance which should result in a lovely supple, swinging way of going.

Each schooling session must begin with a period of loosening up and relaxing the back muscles, however advanced your horse becomes.

It is good to walk on a long rein, as long as your horse is prepared to stretch his head down and walk purposefully. If, on the other hand, he is busy jogging, throwing his head about and shying, such walking will serve no purpose and you might as well start trotting, and then return to walk later on.

This first walk should help him to stretch and loosen up the muscles that have principally tightened because you got on his back, and that anyway have stiffened up while he stood in the stable. Horses who are turned out don't have this problem. Five or ten minutes of active walking with a low head carriage is a good beginning to the day. It also gives you time to think about your own position and to warm up your own muscles. Now pick up a light but steady contact and ask for trot. Work in rising trot.

He will probably vary his rhythm because he has not yet re-discovered the different balance he needs to carry you on his back. In the beginning your first job is to try and discover the right tempo at which to trot. Once this is established you have a better chance of developing rhythm and balance.

You must be very careful, at this stage especially, to rise and sit softly. Your balance is also very important in establishing your horse's rhythm. If you bring your seat back to the saddle a little too quickly you will soon begin to make him hurry to catch up with you. Instead feel the rhythm you want and maintain it with your seat almost as though you were a conductor beating time and making the orchestra keep with you. Every time his steps quicken, steady him, particularly with the feel of your seat, but also with a light rein aid. Just give a momentary squeeze with the outside rein; don't pull backwards in any way.

He may ignore your aids because he finds it simpler to put up with the discomfort of them rather than find out how to adjust his balance. Try to make the corrections principally with your seat and legs and not only with your hands. He will only find his balance when he is properly forward and engaged.

At this stage you must not put strong weight on his back through your seat, but you should keep a steady contact of your lower legs on his sides to keep him forward and therefore, to some extent, engaged. Only when he is consistently more engaged and working through his back will he be able to keep a steady rhythm.

Work on big circles at first as these help him to keep his balance because his inside hind leg is stepping more underneath his body, taking a little more weight. As you change the rein the other hind leg has to work a little harder. Frequent changes of rein from one circle to another will gradually strengthen and develop the hind leg muscles and he will therefore find it easier and easier to carry himself correctly, even on a straight line.

When your horse goes well, don't be tempted to go on for too long. His muscles aren't strong enough for long periods of schooling. Give him plenty of breaks. You can practise making him stand still while you mount and dismount. Another useful and untiring exercise is teaching him to turn, in walk, without the rein contact, just by putting a little more weight on to your inside seat bone.

One of the most difficult problems you are going to experience at this time is teaching your horse that when you ask for more impulsion it doesn't mean faster. Keep your patience and remember that he is trying to learn and to please you. Though the reins are used to control the speed remember that your hands *ask* but *never hold*!

Riding forward to the rein which, on receiving the surge of energy, is briefly squeezed is the basis for the 'half-halt', one of the most valuable aids in the horseman's repertoire.

As your horse begins to discover a better balance you will begin to enjoy a new feeling of control. Another big step up the ladder has been achieved.

CHAPTER NINE

The Contact

In the early stages of dressage riding, getting your horse consistently 'on the bit' will probably seem to be your biggest problem. A skilful rider seldom has any difficulty, while a novice rider can be constantly frustrated in his efforts to overcome his horse's inclination to resist the bit, poke his nose out and carry his head in a way that hollows his back.

As you will have found by reading the previous chapters, it is far more important to concentrate on teaching your horse to work with balance, impulsion and rhythm than to concern yourself with whether or not he is on the bit.

Your hands, the feel they give your horse in his mouth and the way you communicate to him through the rein aids, are a vital link. However, hands alone will not put a horse on the bit, and *no amount of fiddling with the reins* can do anything except make the horse lower his head briefly.

A horse is correctly on the bit only when he is ridden forward with lively activity. The activity of his quarters causes his back to swing and as a result he goes forward into the rein contact. The rider's hands receive that contact and the horse then responds to the energy that is coming from his hind quarters by relaxing his jaw and flexing at the poll.

In the early stages of training, the rider should take a very light contact with the reins. When the time comes to 'put the horse on the bit' the rider must take a more positive rein contact. His hands must always be very sensitive, and, though the feel of the rein has to be a little stronger, the hands must never pull back or restrict. To illustrate the point, imagine that you are holding someone's hand and walking by his side. It is a comfortable feeling for both of you. If you grab someone's hand to stop him going somewhere, you will probably wrench his fingers a little as you pull back. The feeling you should have with your horse is similar: in holding the rein you are holding him by the hand and going along with him.

A horse can accept the bit without being 'on the bit'. When he accepts it he doesn't resent, fight, or try to avoid it. His willingness to accept the bit will probably depend on whether you offer him a good rein contact. From the beginning your horse must learn to accept a light, steady contact with the bit through the reins. Most horses will do this without feeling any apparent discomfort as long as the rider is so well balanced that he can maintain a really 'juicy' contact. Unless your horse accepts the bit it is impossible to develop the activity and rhythm which are necessary to put him 'on the bit'.

You will now see that your position in the saddle is very important to your horse's progress.

Because your arms are attached to your body, if you are out of balance and wobbling about you will almost certainly be moving your hands by mistake. There is no point in trying to keep your hands still if your body is making them move. Even a little stiffness in your back can make your hands bounce.

If your position is supple and balanced you will be able to move your hands quite independently and then you can feel the reins and keep a soft, elastic connection with your horse's mouth.

Generally speaking you should try to maintain the same 'weight' of rein by following all the movements of your horse's head. In walk and canter he moves his head and neck backwards and forwards. In trot he keeps it fairly still, making only small irregular movements rather than rhythmic ones. For this reason it is probably more difficult to keep a good rein contact in trot when there is no rhythmic movement to follow – so you tend to keep your hands totally still.

You may find it rather difficult to understand what is meant by the 'weight' of the rein. Try to imagine that instead of the reins being fastened to the bit they run straight through the bit rings and are fastened to two plastic bags, each containing one or two apples. To prevent the bags from falling on the floor you will have to keep hold of the reins and you will feel a certain weight in your hands. This is rather like the rein contact.

To maintain a good contact your elbow and shoulder joints must be supple and ready to move your hands either forwards or backwards.

Practise keeping the contact in walk and then imagine exactly what the horse is feeling in his mouth. Concentrate on how the reins feel in your hands – whether there are little pulls or jerks – and then imagine a bit in *your* mouth being given the same pulls and jerks! Horses are very long-suffering and they soon become used to all these unintentional jerks, but the trouble is that they can't tell the difference between the unnecessary jerks and the ones that you intend to give: in other words, the rein aids!

If your horse does not accept the bit and is always tossing his head and generally fussing, first make sure that the bit you are using not only fits but is also fitted correctly. If it appears to be correct you should then have his teeth and mouth checked by your veterinary surgeon. Pain could be the reason for apparent naughtiness.

If his back teeth are sharp or rough they could be making the sides of this cheeks sore (rather like when you bite your cheek by mistake), or he might have grown small 'wolf' teeth that appear between his front and back teeth on that part of the jaw where the bit goes. You may not be able to see them because they often stay just under the skin: which is when they are most uncomfortable. Wolf teeth can cause a great deal of pain and they should be taken out.

Young horses sometimes get swollen gums, which can also make them uncomfortable.

Horses often go on growing new back teeth until they are six, and during this period their mouths become very sensitive. If a horse's mouth is sore for any reason it is better not to ride him. Horses have such wonderful memories that they unfortunately remember the unpleasantness of the soreness and go on relating it to having a bit in their mouth. The memory of this pain makes them continue to fuss with their heads long after the soreness has disappeared.

If there is nothing the matter with your horse's teeth or mouth it might be a good idea to try a different kind of snaffle. The one you are using may not fit the shape of his mouth.

Sometimes horses lean on the bit.

A good rein contact has a rather elastic feel, not a dead, heavy one. Some horses are so happy to accept the bit that they also lean on it and you end up practically carrying their heads for them! A horse who does this lacks balance and is finding it by being held up by the reins. With such a horse you must ride him more actively forward up to the rein, which must then soften as he relaxes his jaw.

As your horse works forward into the rein and comes on to the bit he will begin to carry his neck so that his poll is the highest point and there is a gradual curve from withers to poll. When he is young or untrained he will carry his neck rather low, then as he learns to put his hind legs further under his body his neck will become higher. It is the rider's seat and legs that principally determine the deportment of the horse, not his hands.

On the bit.

When you are riding a turn or a circle, the contact should be greater in the outside rein.

A horse who is worked correctly from behind and is not pulled into an outline should not develop faults. However, many horses have been trained incorrectly and unfortunately some have even

been ridden in running reins and have never been given the chance
to use their backs.

OVERBENDING

When a part of the horse's crest and not the poll is seen as the highest
point, the horse is considered to be overbending. It is one of the hard-
est faults of all to correct and is nearly always the result of attempting
to put the horse on the bit by using only the reins.

Overbending.

Correct re-training and sympathetic hands which allow the horse
to stretch his neck *without* losing the contact are the solution.

BEHIND THE BIT

Some horses refuse to go up to the bit, and they bend their necks so
that their nose is behind the vertical (the forehead is further in front
than the nose). The rider is left with a handful of nothing instead of a

ABOVE: *Behind the bit.*

BELOW: *Resisting and dropping behind the bit in walk.*

contact. The more he tries to take a contact the more his horse rolls up his neck and avoids it.

Such a horse must be ridden strongly forward, probably alongside another horse, in a cross-country canter. He must learn to take the bit, and it is difficult to correct this fault in the school. The rider must keep a contact wherever the horse chooses to put his head. Principally he must encourage the horse to stretch forward and down. It is quite ineffective to try and lift the horse's head up by raising your hands. This only makes him go further behind the bit. The line elbow-hand-horse's mouth should be maintained wherever he puts his head. Transitions and school work should be kept to the minimum until the horse begins to go forward willingly.

ABOVE THE BIT

The horse stiffens his jaw, hollows his back and raises his head so that the big muscle under his neck is supporting his head rather than the muscles along the top of his neck and back. He sticks his nose out.

Unfortunately the tendency to go like this often relates to a horse's conformation. Lungeing can help, as long as the side reins are kept fairly low and long. It is, however, impossible to correct the fault with the reins, and only riding actively forward on curved lines, constantly changing direction, will help him to become more supple.

As he learns to flex sideways at the jaw bone and take a proper contact with the outside rein he will begin to come properly on to the bit.

Such faults are principally the result of bad training although poor conformation can also be the cause.

It is very important to remember that you can give yourself many future problems by not taking enough trouble over the simple basic training.

Unfortunately riders do not realise until it is too late that progress in riding can be likened to building a pyramid. It takes a long time to lay the foundations, but the higher you go the quicker it gets. Take time with the early training, and make sure that each stage has been learned correctly.

Perhaps being sure that your horse is going correctly is the most difficult part of all.

One little test you can try – perhaps towards the end of a schooling session – is to let your horse take the reins through your fingers. He should steadily and gradually stretch his head down and push his nose out, looking for the bit. If he doesn't want to do this, it is a sign

ABOVE: *Above the bit.*
BELOW: *Above the bit in halt.*

that he has not been using his back correctly. Though this exercise is easiest in walk or trot it can also be done in canter.

Now you have reached the stage when the paces begin to improve because you are developing real impulsion. Your horse should be becoming more responsive to your aids and you will be able to increase your influence over the way he carries himself.

At this point in your dressage riding career you will have reached and – I hope – taken the right turning at a very important cross roads. However far you travel, success lies at the end of one turning while failure lies at the other. One signpost says: *forward, through a swinging back to your hands*; the other directs you to *pull backwards*.

Have you chosen the right road?

CHAPTER TEN

Turns and Circles

Before you can make further progress you must teach your horse some more aids (signals).

It is important that he now learns to move away, as well as forward, from your leg.

TURN ON THE FOREHAND

In this exercise the horse makes a turn of up to 180° round the foreleg, on the side to which he is turning. One hind leg will cross in front of the other, moving his quarters around his forehand.

Turn on the forehand to the right, showing very good crossing of the hind legs.

This simple exercise is your own first lesson in the absolute necessity of using your aids independently: that is, one hand or leg carrying out one action while the other does something else.

For your horse, obedience to the leg aid which asks him to move sideways is of the greatest importance.

The leg aids are supported by the weight aids. When your horse has been stabled he will already have learned to move over when you touch his side with your hand. If you make it a habit to touch his side, just behind where the girth normally lies, and say 'Over', his understanding of the leg aid will have already begun.

You can now ask for a turn on the forehand from the saddle.

After your normal working-in period, and on a day when everything has gone well and your horse is forward, active, and supple – but not tired – you can teach him the new turn.

You should prepare by bringing him some 3 metres off the track on, say, the left rein, and then halting squarely. The turn you make will be towards the track.

At the halt, bend your horse slightly to the right, but be sure to control the amount of bend with the outside rein (now the left rein). If you fail to keep a proper contact on the outside rein, your horse will

A common error. This rider has used the inside rein to make the turn on the forehand with the result that the horse makes a small circle instead.

walk a small circle! A small squeeze of the right rein should cause the horse to flex at the jaw and yield to the rein aid. If it fails to do so, you must repeat the aid.

Your own weight must not slip to the left; instead, you should have the feeling of lengthening your right leg and putting a little more weight on the right seat bone. Harmonising with the outside (left) rein, the rider's inside leg (right), applied just behind the girth, asks the horse to move his quarters across and around his right foreleg. He may take a hesitant step. Never mind, pat him and encourage him, and then repeat the aid. Your left leg should be behind the girth to stop him swinging round too quickly. This outside leg controls the speed at which the quarters move over and regulates the number of steps.

In the beginning, ask for one sequence of steps at a time and praise him in between.

If you fail to get him to move over, ask for the correct bend again and use your whip. He will soon understand.

His inside (right) hind leg must step in front of his outside (left) hind leg.

As soon as a half turn has been completed, ride actively forward.

This exercise will teach your horse to move away from your leg and will teach you to use independent aids. It should also give you the valuable feel of the outside rein controlling the bend of the horse, and also the knowledge of how to stop his shoulders falling out.

You will use this feel when you are riding turns and circles by riding from your inside leg and seat bone into the outside rein.

LEG YIELDING

There is quite a lot of disagreement about whether leg yielding is a good exercise or not. Carried out in walk and trot it reinforces the obedience to the leg aid that your horse has learned in a turn on the forehand. Neither exercise improves the horse's paces, but they are both good preparation for later movements, and they increase suppleness.

As long as leg yielding is carried out for a few steps only and *correctly*, it has some value.

In leg yielding the horse is required to move forwards and sideways, with his body straight, but with slight flexion at the jaw *away from the direction in which he is travelling*. Both front and hind legs cross, with the inside legs passing in front of the outside legs.

Generally it is best asked for down the long side of the school. On, say, the right rein the horse's hind legs stay on the track while his forehand is well off the track (but his body at not more than 45°). His

This young rider shows leg yielding to the right.

head is bent slightly to the right, and he travels down the track.

Later on you will find that this movement has something in common with shoulder-in, but with one big difference.

The rider starts by making his right (inside) leg long and putting weight on his inside seat bone. His inside leg, close behind the girth, pushes the quarters sideways and forwards.

The use of the outside rein stops the shoulders falling out and the outside leg makes sure that the quarters move calmly and do not rush sideways.

Leg yielding is sometimes used as a preparation for half–pass. It is then ridden across the school with the horse coming off the track, and moving both forwards and across in the direction of the track on the opposite side.

It is much easier for a horse to travel sideways when he is bent away from the direction in which he is travelling. As he gets more supple he finds it easier, and can therefore be straighter. Finally he is able to achieve half-pass, when he must bend *in the direction in which he is travelling.*

If you use this exercise, it is most important for you to remember that your horse should stay in balance. He should not put more weight on one shoulder than the other.

TURNS, LOOPS AND CIRCLES

You may think it rather strange that I have introduced you to some lateral (sideways) movements before explaining about turns and circles and how to ride them correctly.

Unfortunately, it is impossible to ride correctly through a corner if your horse won't bend sufficiently.

Beginning a turn to the left with the pony correctly positioned.

Obviously he is not going to bend round your inside leg, however hard you use it, until he has learned what the correct response is. Never forget that however severely you punish your horse for not obeying you, he *cannot* be expected to understand a lesson that he has not been taught.

Once he has learned to move away from your leg you can quite reasonably expect him to at least try to bend when you ask him on a turn or a curved line.

First, practise turns at the corners of the school, and prepare by positioning yourself and your horse a few metres before the point where your corner will begin. Put your weight a little more on your inside seat bone, with your inside leg stretching down and firmly pressing inwards where it lies. Flex him at the jaw to the inside, with a small take and give of your inside hand, and keep a steady contact on the outside rein. It is very important to have a firmer contact on the outside rein: if this is lost your horse will probably only bend in his neck. Your outside leg should rest a little behind the girth, ready to correct any outward swing of the quarters. This blend of aids should result in your horse instantly bending his body, and flowing easily through the corner.

If he does not bend, you may have pulled back with the reins,

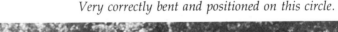

Very correctly bent and positioned on this circle.

or failed to position him correctly before the turn begins. When you put your weight on the inside seat bone make sure that your outside shoulder does not fall behind but stays parallel with your horse's shoulders. Try to feel more weight going on to your inside seat bone as your shoulder moves forward.

If your weight slides to the outside of the saddle when you are turning, it will probably prevent your horse from bending correctly. You must, of course, *never lean inwards*, for this means that you have collapsed your inside hip, and have in fact taken your weight more to the outside of the saddle.

In earlier training you probably spent quite a lot of time riding on large circles. There is nothing wrong with this, for it helps a young horse to find his balance. It also has a very calming effect on a highly strung horse. But the circles you ride must now be improved, and this is achieved by riding with the correct bend, which encourages better balance and, also, much rounder circles.

Changing the rein from right bend (LEFT) to left bend (RIGHT).

This photograph, taken during the warming-up period, shows the horse is not yet really bending through the corner.

A good turn at quite a sharp angle.

Before you begin your circle, make sure your horse is going forward correctly into the reins, and then prepare him as you did for the corner. Ask him to leave the track with the inside rein, then curve his body on the arc of your circle, and ride forward into the outside rein. On the circle, particularly, you should have a secure contact on your outside rein, which controls the degree of bend throughout your horse's body.

A continuous curved line results in a perfect circle; the secret lies in being able to maintain the same bend of your horse throughout the circle, whatever its circumference. The smaller the circle, the greater the bend of the horse.

Do not be tempted to ride very small circles until you can ride larger ones perfectly. Small circles demand far greater suppleness, balance and collection, and asking for them before your horse is physically able to give them to you will result in increased stiffness and general tension.

Great benefit will be gained from riding curved lines, such as loops or serpentines, as long as strict attention is paid to the correct changes of bend. However, be aware that every time you ride an incorrect loop, turn, circle, or whatever, you are letting your horse practise something which is wrong and which can become a bad habit. Unfortunately bad habits are easier to learn than good ones. You must always make corrections. If you fail to correct your horse when you are training, you will certainly not be able to correct him during a test.

STRAIGHTNESS

It is difficult to make your horse straight until he is going forward into the reins, and obedient to the lateral leg aids.

When travelling on a straight line, the horse's hind feet must travel on the same line as his front feet on the same side. His near pair of legs will be on one line, and his off pair of legs on another line. Attention should be paid to this basic straightness from the beginning. Canter can be particularly difficult, with the horse showing a natural tendency to carry his quarters inwards.

Later on you will learn more control of your horse's shoulders, and straightening him will be easier. Now you must concentrate on riding him forward to the outside rein.

I am sure that by now you will have discovered that your horse is much more willing and obedient on one rein than the other. When you are travelling in one direction he lets you keep the contact on the outside rein quite happily and bends willingly to the inside, yet

A horse is straight when his hind legs follow directly behind his front legs.

while going in the other direction he tends to bend to the outside and refuses to be ridden into the outside rein. Don't worry. This is so common that it is normal. Just as humans are left- or right-handed, so horses are more supple in one direction than the other.

Correcting natural stiffness to one side is part of a horse's basic training, and throughout his life he will always find movements in one direction easier than the other. Your job, as a rider and trainer, is to build his muscles so that he is as nearly equal as possible.

Only when you have made him generally more supple, and when he is fully obedient to your forward, lateral and controlling aids, can you really correct his natural crookedness.

Before this is fully possible there are some further lessons which you must both learn. In the meantime, try to make yourself very aware when he is crooked, bent to the outside, or swinging his quarters about, and correct him by riding forward to the outside rein and keeping him straight with your legs.

CHAPTER ELEVEN

Transitions and Halts

I believe that the most important transitions are not changes of pace but transitions that take place *within* the pace – from, say, extended to collected trot or into lengthened strides and back again. The most important transition of all – or perhaps I should say 'aid to transitions' – is the half-halt. This is the dressage rider's most important means of control, and until it is fully understood by both rider and horse, true collection will not be possible.

The half-halt is the essential ingredient to all serious dressage riding. Some people think of it as the icing on the cake. I prefer to think of it as the spoon and the basin in which the cake is made. Without the spoon and the basin there could be no cake.

Poor transitions and halts will lose a lot of marks at Novice level because the tests are short and there is practically a transition or a halt in every movement.

It may seem rather strange, but the solution is not 'practice makes perfect'. In fact if you practise too many transitions you might lose your horse's forwardness. Next time you make a rather bad transition – say from trot to canter – ask yourself whether you had a really good trot before you asked for the change of pace. Generally speaking, and if you are honest with yourself, the answer will be: 'Well, perhaps it wasn't very good.'

Good transitions only happen when your horse is going forward, is correctly on the bit and, most important of all, is well balanced. Transitions have less to do with giving the correct aids than you would imagine.

When you go from a slower pace to a faster one, the moment of change is called an 'upward transition', and from a faster to a slower pace, a 'downward transition'.

Upward transitions require energetic forward willingness from your horse, while downward transitions require your horse to be well prepared and balanced.

Think about sitting in a car. If the driver changes gear and goes forward fast, there will be a sudden jerk that bangs your head against

A transition from rein back to canter.

the back of the seat. The change from slow to fast will feel rather uncomfortable. If the driver changes gears to slow down when he has been going very fast there is an even more horrible jerk and you are thrown forward into your seat belt.

A good driver will accelerate gradually so that his engine is producing more energy, and when he wants to change gear and go faster you will hardly notice the change, because it is so smooth. He will also be careful to reduce speed gradually before he changes into a lower gear.

Like a good driver, a good rider will make sure that his horse is going with enough impulsion before he asks it to go at a faster pace. The forward impulsion ensures that his horse has the energy to re-arrange his feet for the altered sequence of steps, and he then flows forward into the new pace. The good rider will prepare for a transition down by pushing his horse's hind legs a little further underneath him so that that the weight is more on his hind legs. At the same time, and without losing rhythm, he will shorten his strides. This means that the speed at which he is actually travelling will be slower. When the transition is made, the change of speed will be very slight. There should be no jerk, and the horse will not pitch forward and overbalance on to his forehand.

An abrupt transition from canter to halt which resulted in stepping backwards.

When a horse has not had a great deal of training he does not always go with enough impulsion, and he is certainly not always in self-carriage (balance). That is why, in the beginning, before you make a transition up or down you will have to think to yourself: 'Is he going with enough impulsion?', or 'Does he feel balanced enough?'

A young horse can only carry himself with sufficient impulsion and balance for short periods of time. The rider must make sure that transitions are only asked for during those good moments. He must learn to 'prepare' and 'ask' only at the best moments, and to make those best moments happen.

Later on, when your horse is able to sustain his self-carriage, and has learned to go with impulsion, he will begin to be collected. From that point onwards simple transitions should be relatively effortless and the attention to preparation minimal. Only if the balance and impulsion deteriorate, due to the rider's forgetfulness, will there be any difficulties.

Of course, it is not very easy to know just when your horse is really balanced. One of the rider's biggest problems is recognising 'the feel' of when his horse is going correctly. Transitions can be a sort of thermometer for checking this. If you think that your horse is going well, can you ride a good transition? This is one of the occasions when, if you ask your horse a question, he will give you the answer. He will tell you he was going well or incorrectly.

What you must not do is *practise bad transitions*, and though the quality of the pace you are in, and the preparations, are most important, the aids and the way you give them must also be considered.

UPWARD TRANSITIONS

Probably the transitions ridden most are walk-trot. Because they are ridden so frequently we tend to become careless, with the result that many walk-trot, and trot-walk transitions, are sloppily ridden.

With the young horse, the rider should take a contact with the reins in walk but should not ask his horse to 'come correctly on the bit'. At this stage it is sufficient if he simply accepts the bit without dropping it or arguing.

Your inside leg asks for trot with an inward nudge, which is the signal to your horse to change pace. At the same time you must control the first strides into the new pace to make sure that they are not hurried or lazy. This control is most critical. If the walk is not active, your horse may produce a sort of skip forward which is usually the result of a hollow back and hind legs that are not stepping under.

It is also important for the transitions to be obedient. This is the time when you must teach your horse to respond instantly to your aids. A tap with your whip should immediately follow a disobeyed aid to trot. Only when the horse really starts to listen can you perfect your transitions. Don't nag with your legs whatever you do. An unwilling, unresponsive transition will never be a good one.

You have to feel, under your seat, when your horse is going with sufficient energy to be asked to trot. Then, as he moves into the next pace you must keep that steady rein contact, neither pulling back, nor lightening the feel in your hands.

The secret of transitions is not to change the feel in your horse's mouth. If you resort either to pulling back or fixing your hands your horse will not be free to use his head and neck. If he is unable to use them he will not be able to balance. It is like running fast with your hands tied behind your back. You will probably be able to run, but you won't be able to do it to the best of your ability.

A lot of people are aware of this problem, and in trying to help their horse as much as possible they tend to give the reins away! This is unhelpful to the horse, for he is accustomed to looking for the bit and if it is not there he will go towards it. In other words, he will stretch his head forward and down and will change his balance.

The more in harmony you are and the less moving you do during a transition, the better. Always try to refine your aids: that is, make them as small as possible.

Ideally your horse will walk actively, accepting the bit. As you give the aid to trot he will step forward smoothly, and with absolutely clear steps, into trot. There will be no shuffling. There should be no loss of balance and within two or three strides the full freedom of the stride should be established. From the very first steps the rhythm must not vary.

This seems a great deal to think about. In simple terms: it means finding the right amount of energy and then controlling it.

TROT TO CANTER

The aids which I suggest here are the ones most commonly used. Please do not worry if you are taught different ones. It is quite acceptable to ask in a different way.

With a young horse it is better to ask for canter just before a corner.

To canter with the right leg leading, make sure that your trot is active and swinging along. Ask yourself whether it feels as though you could canter easily. It is essential for your horse to work correctly through his back and into the reins. If he is fussing or resistant in any way *don't ask for canter* but correct the trot first.

Keep your right (inside) leg on the girth and make sure that your horse is slightly flexed to the right. Two strides before the corner, brush your left (outside) lower leg back, so that your horse can feel it moving. The strike-off is asked for by a combination of the outside leg aid and the inside seat bone being weighted and slightly pushed forward. Some books of instruction ignore the weighting of the inside seat bone – certainly any horse can be taught to canter on a correct leg without it. However, if you are ambitious as a dressage rider, you must prepare your horse for the future, and good flying changes of leg only come from changes ridden from the seat bones. The leg aid will soon become secondary.

The rein contact must be maintained throughout the transition, with your horse taking more contact with the outside rein. The hands *must* go with the movement of his head and neck, but it is equally important for the outside rein to stay in good contact; otherwise he will fall on to his outside shoulder and will almost certainly strike off on the wrong leg.

If you have problems getting the correct strike-off, ask yourself:

Was my horse positioned correctly for the corner?

Did I keep the contact of the outside rein?
Was the trot forward?
Did I ask correctly?
Was my weight in the right place or did I either slide to the outside of the saddle, or lean forward and look down at the horse's leg that should be leading?

If you feel you have done everything correctly, come back quietly to trot, without upsetting your horse, and ask again.

If there is repeated disobedience it is either because your horse genuinely doesn't understand or because he is very stiff to one side and finds cantering on one lead too difficult – or possibly even painful.

In either case, don't snatch him back into trot or he may begin to think it is wrong to canter at all!

Instead, continue to canter with the wrong lead on a big circle. He will probably break into trot because he will also find this – cantering with the wrong lead very difficult. If he does, simply apply the correct canter aids again, and perhaps this time you will be lucky. When he does respond correctly, keep cantering in as big a circle as is possible and make a great fuss of him, either with your voice or a caress. Make this canter as pleasant and simple for him as you can. Taking your weight out of the saddle will make it easier for him. Let him really enjoy himself, then quietly bring him back to walk, through trot, and let him walk on a long rein. This gives him time to have a think about what you have asked and what he has done.

If you've had a real problem over a particular lead and finally achieved it, do as I suggest above but don't repeat the exercise again on that day. If you do, you might have to stop on a bad note instead of a good one.

TROT TO WALK

Downward transitions are the stepping stone to half-halts, but only if they are ridden correctly. It is essential for them to be ridden with the seat and legs and never with hands that pull back or fix.

The trot must be active, but before you ask for the walk transition it is necessary to increase the engagement of your horse's hind legs so that there is less weight on his forehand. The lighter he is in front, the easier it will be for him to make a good transition.

To achieve increased lightness the rider should close his legs and ride forward from his seat without allowing his horse to change rhythm. The energy he generates should be received into quiet, receptive hands; there is a split second when the contact of both reins is stronger, then, as the horse walks, the hands yield. If the horse does not respond, repeat the sequence. *On no account start pulling.*

The rider must be ready for the slightest offer of walk from the horse and should be ready to accept it and to allow his horse to take forward, clear, walk steps straight away.

Any holding, fixing, or pulling back will only result in a stiff back and shuffling or jogging steps.

The moment the rider feels the transition being offered, his whole body should soften and receive the new pace, while his hands follow the movement of the horse's head.

At the beginning you must be prepared for a certain lack of success. When you get a good response, be generous in your praise. When there is a lack of understanding, be patient yourself and stay calm.

Don't make the mistake of dropping the reins as soon as you move into walk. Always ask for at least a few steps of walk, with your horse taking the contact of the rein. If you always give him complete freedom as soon as he walks he will go on expecting it!

CANTER TO TROT

There is very little difference in the aids for a transition from canter to trot, to a transition from trot to walk. The rein aids are very slight, and the rider's body tends to be all that is needed to produce a transition to trot. The rider, however, will find this transition more difficult because his balance is more easily disturbed as he comes from canter to trot.

To begin with, transitions are best ridden on a circle or just before a corner.

Cantering on a circle increases the engagement of the inside hind leg, so horses are more balanced. Riding towards a corner makes the horse balance himself.

Make sure that the canter is energetic and springy, with your horse as well engaged as possible. When you feel that he is well balanced, just relax your seat muscles and slightly squeeze, the outside rein. On no account should you keep holding, or your horse will lean on your hands and, of course, will fall on to his forehand as he trots. Instead, squeeze, and follow the movement of his head, which in the beginning can be considerable. At all costs maintain the same contact and keep your own balance.

You will only be able to do this if you let your body flow with your horse's movements. Be ready to ride the rhythm into the trot immediately.

THE HALT

It is only possible to ride good halts after your horse has learned half-halts. For this reason I am putting how to ride them into the next chapter.

A good halt should result in your horse standing squarely and well

A straight, square halt.

Fairly square, but a little above the bit into halt.

balanced between his four legs, on the bit, and waiting for your instructions. Any other type of halt does not come into the category of halt required in a dressage test. I prefer to call any other type of halt a 'stop'! (There will be much more about understanding a dressage test, and how you are meant to ride it, later on in this book.)

There are two categories of transition: 'direct' and 'progressive'. A progressive transition – say walk to canter – may be made through a few steps of trot. A direct transition – walk to canter – may not have any trot steps. In the early stages of a horse's training, all transitions are ridden progressively, including trot to halt, which may show two or three walk steps before the horse actually halts.

Working on transitions will certainly help your horse to find his balance, but they must be ridden forwards. Any tendency for your horse to start dropping the bit or thinking 'backwards' must be guarded against.

Transitions must always be ridden forwards by increasing the aids to bring the horse's centre of gravity closer to his hind legs.

CHAPTER TWELVE

Half-Halt and Halt

To be able to understand why it is necessary to teach your horse the half-halt it is important to understand its value and why it plays such an important part in horsemanship.

Its name doesn't really explain its full function. To me a half-halt sounds just about like a half-stop or a hesitation.

It is certainly neither of these.

The well-executed half-halt shifts the horse's weight, in a second, further on to his hind quarters in an almost invisible way. It draws together the horse's forward energy, thereby putting it to its maximum effect.

This may seem like a hesitation, so a better word might be 're-grouping'. Hesitation implies indecision. A half-halt is quite the opposite. It is like taking a deep breath before doing something difficult. Think of yourself running down a hill which becomes steeper, and finding yourself going faster and faster. Unless you choose to keep running until you reach the bottom – and you might fall over if you do – you will have to make a big effort and throw your weight back for a half-halt, thereby re-balancing yourself.

Watch any top athlete who throws or hits a ball. Before the throw or hit there is always a moment of near stillness. During it, all the available power is gathered together and poised at the most efficient point of balance for whatever is to follow.

This is what you are trying to achieve with the horse. You want to place him, and his full power, in the best possible position to carry out what you know will be a difficult movement. Hesitation would lose his energy. Instead, you are asking him to draw it together and rebalance himself.

When a horse knows he has something difficult to do he automatically makes a half-halt. Because he does it naturally it is fluent and almost invisible. If when watching racing on TV you have seen a loose horse jumping a large fence in slow motion, you will have noticed how dramatically he moved his weight on to his hind quarters in the stride before take-off.

In dressage you are asking for great obedience. When your horse has to do a difficult movement, such as a canter pirouette, the only way you can warn him that something is about to happen is to give him a signal. *You* have to tell him to prepare himself, because otherwise he will have no warning. You therefore use the half-halt.

In dressage, the half-halt is more than just a preparation for a difficult movement. It is the way in which you develop your horse's collection as well as the way in which you remind him that he must listen to you. It also prepares him for a transition, and regulates the pace. If at any time there is a loss of balance, such as when your horse is leaning on the bit, a half-halt will come to your rescue.

To sum up, a half-halt is a fleeting moment when the rider's aids say 'prepare'. As a result, the horse momentarily gathers himself and puts his weight further towards his hind quarters. He is telling you: 'I am ready.' Through bending the joints of his hind leg he lowers his quarters, thus shifting and taking the increased weight from his forehand.

Though this half-halt seems, and is, a universal answer to many problems, it is not magic. Your horse has to systematically learn how to do it. It takes months for him really to understand what you want him to do, and even then he can only partly accomplish what you ask of him because he is not yet muscularly powerful enough.

Constant attention and frequent practice will bring positive results if you, the rider, are patient, rewarding, and not too demanding.

The aids for the half-halt are: both legs closed to send the horse forward; rider pushes his tummy forwards while he deepens his seat and stretches his legs down. As a result, the horse should go more firmly into the reins and at this moment the rider must have a non-allowing hand: that is, he closes his fingers, does not keep the same contact, but allows his horse to increase the weight in the rein. The very moment that the rider feels the extra weight in his hands – and, it is hoped, a response in his horse, he must relax and release the increased weight in the reins. This is the vital part.

In the beginning there can be confusion, especially if the rider doesn't have very sensitive hands. Too much leg will make your horse pull and lean on the reins. Too much seat will make him hollow his back and resist right through his body.

It must be rather bewildering for a horse to be asked to go forward only to find his is being stopped, but the quick reaction of the rider, who is able to feel the briefest response from his horse and *react instantly* by yielding, should quickly overcome the muddle in his mind.

If during training the rider finds no response, or – even worse – positive resistance, he must *repeat* the aids rather than increase them.

Only when your horse is reasonably established in a basically correct way of going – that is, with a good rhythm, reasonable balance, and above all a supple, swinging back and relaxed poll – can the half-halt be introduced. The essential of the half-halt is that it goes right through the horse. This will be impossible if he is working in a restricted way. Unless he is soft and free, the aids for the half-halt would result in paralysing stiffness. Nothing but failure can result in starting before the horse is ready.

The first introduction to the aids are made in trot-walk-trot transitions. Apply the correct aids and, the moment your horse walks, ask him to go forward. To make a successful downward transition the horse has to put more weight on his hind legs: so this becomes a first step on the ladder to a correct half-halt. Make sure that the transitions are clear and that the first walk steps are free and forward.

A split second after a half-halt.

As soon as the walk is going forward with purpose, your horse can be ridden forwards again into trot – now, it is hoped, with his hind legs a little further underneath him.

It is better to teach the aids in this way rather than within the pace. If it is attempted within the pace before the aids are understood it is very easy to spoil the horse's correct way of going.

Once your horse has fully understood these aids, and if over a period of time the exercises have often been repeated, they can be introduced during trot. The rider applies the aids, and the moment he feels the horse preparing himself for the expected walk transition he must relax his aids and send him forward. The slightest response must be quickly rewarded and then the lesson should be brought to an end. Soon it will be visible that at the moment the half-halt is made the horse lowers his quarters. When this begins to happen you should be able to feel a slight rounding of your horse's back under your seat and there will be a related softening in his jaw and poll which you will feel in your fingers.

This is a wonderful moment, for he is giving you his full attention and his body is ready to do as you ask.

The more effective the response to your half-halt aids, the greater will be your overall influence.

The better your horse understands, the smaller and more refined your aids can become.

Great patience will reward you finally with success and a new dimension will be added to the pleasure of riding.

THE HALT

Once both you and your horse begin to understand the half-halt you will find that your halts improve considerably.

The full halt is generally only ridden on straight lines.

In a good halt your horse will stand straight, square and still, his legs pair by pair abreast of each other.

He will remain on the bit, balanced and attentive, his poll being the highest point. The transition into and out of the previous pace must be smooth.

This quality of the halt is only likely to be achieved if, through a half-halt, your horse is properly prepared and ridden forward until he is still. Even during the halt there will be an element of forward riding: in other words, you must stay at attention yourself.

In lower level tests, when making the transition, a few steps of walk are generally accepted by the judge. At higher levels, when the preceding pace is either trot or canter, the transition is expected to be direct – that is without any interrupting steps of another pace in between. The better the halt, the smoother and lighter the transitions will be.

The principal problems you will have with halts will be crookedness, lack of squareness, and a predominant lack of balance.

Crookedness is usually the result of your horse not going forward correctly into your reins, while the lack of squareness and balance depends for correction very much on a half-halt preparation. It is generally the unbalanced horse who stands with his feet in a muddle and his weight leaning one way or another. Through standing in such a way he will also find it impossible to stay on the bit, remain attentive to your aids, and be ready to move forward.

When the halt is crooked and not square or properly balanced, the move-off is going to be difficult.

To ask for halt the rider first makes a half-halt and then repeats the same aids more definitely for a full halt. Only by remembering to continue to use the forward aids until the halt is established will the halt be good.

The rider himself must remain alert throughout the halt and his hands must allow any small movements of his horse's head.

In early training, halts must be gradual and your horse given a little time to arrange himself. As training progresses the halt will become more direct until, finally, the canter to halt will be possible.

CHAPTER THIRTEEN

Understanding and Improving the Paces

As long as you feel that your horse's all-important basic training, as described in the preceding chapters, is correct, then he is ready for further progress.

I hope I have explained this early training well enough for you not to feel that it is too complicated. If you haven't understood and you don't feel that you have accomplished suppleness, rhythm, forwardness, and obedience to your aids, don't automatically blame yourself. I may have explained badly, or your horse might be being difficult. In either case, seek help from someone else before you attempt to go further.

The time has now come to improve your horse's paces. This is the whole object of dressage. You are now at the point where the patience and time you have taken teaching your horse how to carry your weight on his back, and allowing him to learn obedience to your aids without upsetting his confidence, are going to start paying you back richly.

There are four trots:

WORKING TROT

This is the pace you have been using. It is closest to the horse's natural trot, but through training has become a little more energetic and lively. This is the pace you will always use when you are warming up or riding out in the countryside. It is comfortable for you and your horse.

MEDIUM TROT

This is a little more demanding. The steps must be longer and rounder as a result of more obvious impulsion coming from your horse's hind

Medium trot.

quarters. It is essential for the rhythm not to change. The extra energy should not result in a loss of balance, but your horse must be allowed to lengthen his whole frame slightly. He must keep the same rhythm and stay on the bit.

The often-asked-for movement, 'lengthened strides', is the preliminary to developing a true medium trot.

Working and medium trot are the bases for developing and improving your horse's trot, though during his earlier training you will only lengthen the strides a little. As your horse develops his ability to move to and from working trot, so the joints of his legs will start to bend energetically, adding life and spring to his trot. The increased energy will flow through his back, and his shoulders will seem to grow in front of you, with his neck becoming more raised.

It is only possible to start lengthening and shortening the strides when your horse is strong enough to accept the half-halt aids. In the earlier stages it is enough to ask for a few steps of more active trot while you make sure that he keeps his balance and rhythm. After a few months of correct training, your horse should be strong enough to accept you in sitting trot. Until he is happy with you sitting it is not really possible to make progress, for you need the positive contact of your seat in the saddle.

It is important to understand that a great deal of harm can be done by forcing your horse to accept you in sitting trot before his back muscles are strong enough. But it is equally easy to imagine you are doing the right thing by staying in rising trot for too long. The time comes when your young horse must accept your weight in the saddle and respond to the weight aids. Too much delay is a mistake.

Once your horse can stay balanced and rhythmic in sitting trot and keep his lovely soft, swinging stride, he is ready to learn the half-halt. Making transitions smoothly from working trot to medium and back again with repetition will also develop greater elastic suppleness. Throughout such transitions the rhythm must be protected by continuous attention. Rhythm is fundamental to the quality of the trot.

At all times loss of balance and consequent falling on to the fore-hand must be carefully guarded against. A horse who is on his fore-hand cannot improve his trot.

It is the increased bounce and swing of the trot that will improve the whole feel of the pace.

If you think principally about keeping an unhurried rhythm and a truly energetic, elastic impulsion, you will make progress, I am sure.

Your body must 'conduct' the rhythm of the beats and you must make sure that your 'orchestra' (horse) stays in harmony with you.

The two other trots belonging to a more advanced stage of training are:

COLLECTED TROT

The horse moves with more energy, while his hind legs carry a greater proportion of the weight. He moves with shorter steps than in the other trots, and as a result his steps are very light and springy and his shoulders are free. Because of the positioning and activity of his hind legs his back swings, his quarters lower, and his head and neck become more raised.

Most people do not try to develop the collected trot until their horses have fully understood and are able to carry out the half-halt. The progressive use of the half-halt, when the horse gradually learns

Collected trot.

to put more weight, briefly, on his hind legs, with the corresponding bending of their joints, results in muscle development. To ask for collection before the muscles have developed will merely result in shorter steps, not an active, lively impulsion.

EXTENDED TROT

This is the most forward, biggest striding trot that your horse can make. It requires great activity, balance and spring. It is only correctly developed as a result of collection.

Maintaining the same rhythm, your horse covers as much ground as possible by lengthening his strides to the maximum.

Extended trot. Note the greater activity of the hind and forelegs.

As a result of these powerful strides, marked by the hind feet imprints coming well over the imprints of the fore feet, the whole frame of the horse must lengthen.

If the power for the strides doesn't come from the greater activity of his hind legs, you may find that he is leaning on the bit and losing his balance.

A rather unnatural, 'flicking' toe action of the front legs is faulty and is usually the result of a lack of powerful activity from the quarters or from a stiff, tense back.

There are four canters:

WORKING CANTER

Just as the working trot is the 'everyday' trot, the same applies to the working canter.

In the beginning it will feel very unbalanced and uncontrolled.

Gradually, as your horse finds his balance and moves his weight more to his hind quarters, the whole feeling will change. The three beats of the canter will be clearly felt, followed by a silent beat when all his feet are off the ground together. He will land lightly on the ground, his steps will be regular and unhurried, and he will remain confidently on the bit. There must always be impulsion, for without it the canter will lack spring and may become a four-beat canter. This is a serious fault.

As you read earlier in this book, one hind foot and one forefoot come to the ground together. If there is a marked lack of energy from the horse, the hind foot may come to the ground before the forefoot which is normally its pair. This happens when the hind legs are left so far behind that they are forced to touch the ground first, thus making the four separate beats.

In early training you should not attempt to make your horse canter too slowly. If you do this before he has established a correct balance and rhythm he will be forced to stiffen. Instead, try to have the feeling that he is springing into the air with each stride and giving you the feeling of riding uphill.

Canter should not be asked for until you are confident that your horse understands the aids and is obedient in trot. In the very early stages it is often better to canter with a light seat: that is, with your weight taken on to your stirrups. This allows your horse to round his back and bring his hind legs 'through' underneath him. Gradually, you can rest your seat softly in the saddle, and by moving at the hip joint and in the spine – the tummy being pushed forward as your horse takes the weight on to his forelegs – you will find that you can regulate the flow of the movement. Your seat muscles must remain soft and your seat should stay in continuous contact with the saddle. Any tension in the rider causes the canter stride to shorten and hurry.

Just as in the trot, you must make your body 'conduct' the rhythm and speed of the canter. With a young horse you should almost feel that your seat is slowly stroking the horse. Life and impulsion in the stride should be encouraged. If any attempt is made to force the pace the natural expression will soon be lost.

It is very important for you to feel your inside leg stretching down and a slight increase of weight on your inside seat bone. In canter it is all too easy to be pushed to the outside of the saddle.

Long periods of canter are not a good idea; your young horse will find it too difficult to sustain enough balance and energy. Far more will be gained by cantering twice round the school and then making a transition to trot. The exercise can be repeated, but not so quickly that your horse feels he is being corrected for doing something wrong.

A circle in trot, while you tell him how clever he is, followed by a further short period of canter, will do far more good than a prolonged canter.

Later on, in place of transitions you can make half-halts to improve the pace. Eventually his balance will be so good that you will achieve canter-to-walk with ease. It is all a gradual process that cannot be hurried.

Throughout all canter training, great attention should be paid to straightness. In the very early stages you may not be able to make any corrections. As more impulsion, obedience, and the acceptance of your aids are accomplished you will be able to keep a good contact of the outside rein and place the horse's shoulders in front of his hind quarters. This is the best way of correcting crookedness, and is more effective than trying to move his quarters.

MEDIUM CANTER

In medium canter the horse should lengthen his strides without changing rhythm. He must be well balanced and the rider must again feel that he is 'going uphill'. Any tendency to fall on to the forehand should be corrected by returning to working canter and re-balancing it. Ideally the steps will be longer and more springy and will cover more ground.

Medium canter.

COLLECTED CANTER

Collection should only be introduced when your horse has learned all his early lessons. It should certainly be a year before you begin to introduce even a suggestion of collection.

In collected canter the steps are shorter and more active. The forehand becomes very light and the shoulders free and mobile. The horse must be very supple throughout his body so that the increase in the activity and engagement of his hind quarters results in a flow of controlled energy and a light acceptance of the bit. As a result of this engagement, his neck will be more raised and arched.

EXTENDED CANTER

Though it is good for the young horse to enjoy a 'strong canter' out on a ride, an extended canter should not be asked for until his training is much further advanced.

In the extended canter the horse covers as much ground as possible by taking really long strides without losing rhythm. He must not fall

Extended canter. Note the greater activity.

on to his forehand, but must remain light and calm. He must remain on the bit while at the same time lengthening his frame.

WALK

The walk is the easiest of all the paces to spoil, therefore it is very important for you to know exactly what it should be like. Only if you really understand what is correct and what is incorrect can you guard against future problems.

In the beginning the young horse feels very wobbly with you on his back and finds it very difficult to walk straight. He is probably a bit crooked naturally, anyway. If he is tense or walks in an aimless way it is very easy for him to learn to step unevenly.

I am repeating again the sequence of steps because *it is so important for you to know and feel them*: right hind – right fore – left hind – left fore. Equal time should be spent on each leg and the beats must be absolutely four-time. The hind legs and the forelegs should be placed and lifted in the same way. For example, the near hind should be picked up and put down in the same relative position as the off hind. It is a common fault for one leg to be placed further under the body of the horse than the other.

The worst fault in walk is when the horse moves the fore and hind legs on the same side forward at the same or almost the same moment. This movement, when two beats only are heard or felt, is termed an 'amble'. The fore and hind legs on the same side should not be seen to move in the same direction at the same time.

In a correct walk, the split second before the hind leg is placed on the ground the foreleg is lifted up. If you watch a good walk carefully you will see that a V is formed by the legs at this moment.

Another severe fault is when the rhythm becomes broken and instead of being clearly 1–2–3–4–1–2–3–4 it becomes 1–2——3–4——1–2——3–4. It feels half way to becoming a jog.

The rider should be constantly alert to the dangers of these faults. He must learn what a correct walk feels like and through that understanding must preserve the true walk which nature gave his horse. It is riders, not horses, who spoil the paces. Instead, it must be our duty and our joy to improve them.

Many good trainers will only walk on a long rein for the first year of a horse's life. Others believe that the horse should accept the contact and work in medium walk. It will always remain a matter of individual choice and will also be partially dependent on the type of walk that your horse has. Those with a naturally big walk often lack co-ordination and, although they have the potential to finally show the best walk, they can be the most difficult in their early years. They simply cannot get their front legs out of the way quickly enough.

To be safe, and unless your trainer suggests otherwise, work for the first year on a long rein in a free walk: that is, with as much rein as the horse will take without having a loop in the reins. When you want to give your horse a complete rest you can give him a loose rein, which means you are riding almost on the buckle.

Walking over poles about 3 feet apart can help to improve the walk.

Even in the free walk you must be very careful that the steps remain correct. The best time for practising the walk is out on a ride, when your horse becomes more naturally active and is interested in seeing what is round the next corner. Because of this, his steps are purposeful and forward and he develops the habit of a good walk rather than a bad one. You may sometimes need to take up the contact, which is quite acceptable for short periods.

Gradually, as your horse accepts the forward aids and accepts the bit in trot and canter you will find that, in about his second year of training, you will be able to pick up the contact and begin to walk him on the bit in medium walk.

I believe that a horse's walk can be spoiled by the rider rocking from side to side and causing a slight loss of balance. This is a common riding fault, especially with a relaxed rider who tends to collapse first one hip and then the other with the motion of the walk. This accentuates the horse's problem with his balance.

FREE WALK

The horse should walk actively, with long purposeful strides. This is considered a pace of rest and he must be allowed complete freedom to lower and stretch out his head and neck.

MEDIUM WALK

This is the normal walk on the bit. It should be calm, energetic and regular. Generally, the hind feet will touch the ground just in front of the footprints of the forefeet. This varies a good deal, however, and is largely dependent on the natural length of the horse's stride, combined with the length of his back. Obviously a long back keeps the hind legs further from the front ones, and less overtrack is therefore possible. The horse should remain on the bit while the rider maintains a light, steady contact.

COLLECTED WALK

Another word of warning. Your progress towards collected walk must be gradual. This walk is very difficult to achieve and must evolve slowly. Any attempt to make it collected with the hands is doomed. It has to be a slow progress achieved principally through the rider developing his sense of feel to a much higher degree than is necessary in the other paces. It is particularly difficult to judge just how much energy is required, and a common mistake is not to have enough. However, energy does *not* mean quick steps. Because there is no spring in the walk, as compared to the trot and canter, the rider finds it much harder to find the right ingredients.

Each horse is very individual in his ability to sustain collected walk but, generally speaking, the walk *follows the other paces*. In other words, your horse must be working well on the bit in trot and canter before he begins medium walk, and he must be showing collection and extension in trot and canter before he is asked for the same in walk.

In collected walk the steps must be *higher* and shorter. The hind feet touch the ground behind, or just in, the print of the forefoot. The joints are more flexed and the neck is raised higher, depending on how much collection has been achieved. Activity is more marked, there should be a light acceptance of the bit, with the horse's face being slightly in front of or approaching the vertical.

EXTENDED WALK

The horse lengthens his strides as much as he can, covering as much ground as possible without hurrying. A light contact must be maintained while the horse is allowed to stretch his head and neck. The hind feet must step well over the print of the forefeet.

The extended walk is the natural development of the medium walk. The freedom of the strides, whilst accepting the bit, will grow from the medium walk and the free walk.

The paces will improve as long as they are not forced. It is the rider who must know what his objectives are and must learn the speed at which he should travel towards them.

Always remember that when new skills have to be learned new muscles have to be developed.

CHAPTER FOURTEEN

Thinking about Collection and Lateral Work

Collection is not something that is suddenly learned by your horse. It is a process that begins the first time he is backed and goes on developing right through his training until he is so superbly balanced that he can trot on the spot (piaffe) and almost canter on the spot (canter pirouettes).

The most difficult movements of dressage are introduced gradually as your horse improves his balance. However, movements such as shoulder-in, half-pass and counter canter will, through their use, *increase his ability to collect himself.*

Throughout training, you will be gradually increasing the degree of difficulty of exercises: *but no faster than your horse is able to develop the necessary muscles and physical stamina to carry out the new exercises.* If you try to progress too quickly, the horse will experience a real discomfort that amounts to pain. He is then bound to resist and to resent what you are asking him to do. But if you progress at the right speed he will experience only the slight discomfort that is really no more than increased effort.

So we have a rather 'which came first, the chicken or the egg?' situation. Before you can do shoulder-in and half-pass types of exercise you have to develop some collection. Yet those very same exercises are designed and used to increase your horse's ability to improve the collection which he already has. You have to feel your way a little, and this is where experience counts.

So far, you will have been able to learn most of the points in this book with a combination of theory (reading) and practice (lessons). From here onwards, although you can certainly learn the principles and the reasoning yourself, teaching your horse will be difficult without sustained help from an experienced trainer.

WHAT IS COLLECTION?

When a horse is collected he is carrying himself in such a balanced way that he is ready to do whatever is required of him, whether it be jumping forward into gallop to piaffe, or to show extended trot.

Compare him with a human athlete. A top-class tennis player waiting for a serve stands bouncing on the balls of his feet, ready to go backwards, forwards or to either side, whichever way is necessary. A fencer must always be in perfect balance. A ballet dancer or a gymnast clearly demonstrates the importance of perfect balance.

You will have often felt yourself preparing, even for something easy like jumping over a narrow stream, by gathering your energy and drawing yourself together.

Your horse does not know when you are going to ask him to do movements that require increased balance and energy, so you have to train him, through your aids, to 'collect himself together' when he is told to.

With a young horse who has not yet learned the aids, you may feel him 'gathering himself together' when he gets excited. He may make some very short, bouncy trot steps, or may even piaffe. Occasionally you may feel that he is practically cantering on the spot. This is a sort of natural collection. He is getting himself ready to join in some fun or even to run away from something frightening. The top-class gymkhana pony, for example, has taught himself how to put his hind legs well enough underneath his body in order to stop and turn at incredible speed.

At these moments, you feel the great power of the horse underneath you. If it is a spontaneous and uncontrollable feeling, it can be a little frightening. But when it is in obedience to your aids it is the most wonderful feeling imaginable.

True collection is achieved when the horse's hind legs step forward towards his body and under the centre of his gravity. As they step more towards him, so more weight is taken on to his hind legs. As the weight *is taken on to the hind leg so the hip, stifle and hock joints bend.*

As a result, the rider will feel the quarters lower and the forehand lighten. This gives the shoulders great freedom to move. The horse becomes very controllable yet very active.

Any attempt to impose collection on your horse by force through the hands will produce a stiff back and stiff hind legs. Such riding is the enemy of collection.

Suppleness and swing must never be lost sight of, and when real collection is attained the flow of energy through the swinging back will be uninterrupted.

Collected paces have shorter but higher steps; lower, more engaged

Passage – a very collected, elevated, springy trot.

Piaffe – the greatest degree of collection. Note the lowered hind quarters. The horse is so balanced and collected that he is able to trot on the spot.

quarters; and impulsion that ripples through the horse and takes him forward. The horse should be in perfect balance and will not need to support himself through the contact of the reins in the rider's hands.

WHY GO SIDEWAYS?

Going sideways is known as 'lateral work'. There are many different exercises which ask the horse to step sideways with the fore and hind legs. These exercises are considered so important in the training of the horse that they form part of dressage tests at various levels. Without lateral exercises it would be very hard to develop real collection.

In Chapter 10, *Turns and Circles*, I explained the importance of teaching your horse to move away from your leg. This was a very important early lesson.

SHOULDER-IN

This is perhaps the most valuable single exercise for either a horse or his rider.

When you really understand how to ride shoulder-in you will suddenly discover another dimension of control. When you are able to control your horse's shoulders – turns, circles and keeping him straight will become much easier. If you did not believe in the importance of riding into the outside rein from your inside leg you will certainly start wishing that you had done so now!

Shoulder-in is generally ridden down the long side of the school, though it may be ridden almost anywhere, including on a circle.

The horse's shoulders are brought in off the track while his hind legs remain on it. His body is bent as equally as possible to the inside and therefore *away from the direction in which he is travelling*.

The inside front leg will cross the outside front leg, while the inside hind leg should be placed well forward under the belly and towards the outside front leg.

In the beginning, shoulder-in will be performed on three tracks: that is, with the outside hind leg on the first track, the inside hind and the outside fore on the second track, and the inside foreleg on the third track. Later on, the shoulder-in may be performed on four tracks, in which case each leg makes a track of its own. The tracks should be spaced equally apart.

Before you begin, do try to get a clear picture in your mind of exactly what you are attempting.

Shoulder-in.

The FEI rule book states that the shoulder-in should be performed at an angle of about 30° to the direction in which the horse is moving.

Don't be put off by all these technical words. Shoulder-in is really very easy as long as you don't try too hard. Most of the problems can be avoided if you allow your horse to stay supple and rhythmic.

If you can practise on an experienced horse it will be a great help. If, however, you and your horse are learning together it may be better to start in walk, even though the exercise is usually carried out in trot, because it gives you both time to think.

Your natural instinct will be to use the inside instead of the outside rein. Try to remember that your horse's legs are under his shoulders and that you can only control the shoulders with the outside rein.

Riding shoulder-in is a bit of a knack, so don't worry if you find it difficult at first.

The best way to begin your first attempt at shoulder-in is by making a 10-metre circle: say on the right rein, just at the corner of the long side. Make sure that your horse is walking actively, bending corectly around your inside leg, and taking the contact of the outside rein. As you meet the longside track, keep the outside rein contact and fractionally move your hand towards the neck, almost bringing the shoulder inwards within the rein. This is a very sensitive movement. Too much rein will only cause resistance or bring the shoulder in so far that your horse will lose balance and rhythm. Keep the lightness of the inside rein, and, at the precise moment that you feel the shoulders move a little off the track, use your inside leg to remind your horse to go forward actively down the track while keeping the same angle.

In a nutshell, you are guiding the forehand off the track with the outside rein whilst maintaining impulsion and forward movement with your inside leg. Your inside hand maintains a very light contact that gives small reminders to your horse to keep the bend. Your outside leg will be ready, behind the girth, to correct any swing of the quarters.

If you encounter problems don't apply stronger aids. Instead, make them lighter, and you might well be surprised by the good results.

Ask someone to watch you, in order to make sure that you are not asking for too much angle. Remember to keep your weight slightly on your inside seat bone. Above all, don't pull with the inside rein; this results in too much bend in the neck and no shoulder-in.

As soon as you achieve the magic feeling of being able to move your horse's shoulders with the outside rein in both directions, try it in trot. Though it may seem more difficult for you, it is easier for your horse, because in that moment of spring, crossing his front legs is less effort, since he is airborne.

When you make shoulder-in in trot you must make sure that you shorten the strides a little. This is when it becomes necessary to ask for a slight degree of collection.

Some riders make a small circle in preparation; not only does this confirm that the horse is bending correctly and is into the outside rein but also, in order to remain in balance on a small circle, he will naturally shorten his steps.

If you can manage without the circle, do so. If it helps at first, use it.

To begin with, be satisfied with just a few steps, especially if your horse has stayed balanced and supple. Reward him by riding forward on to a curved line, which is the easiest thing you can ask him to do. Later on, you must teach him to straighten by bringing his shoulders once again in line with his hind legs. He is generally required to do this in a test.

The worst faults that can occur in shoulder-in are failing to bring the forehand off the track because the horse is putting too much weight on his outside shoulder through having his neck bent inwards; or losing rhythm and suppleness because the impulsion and balance are disturbed.

Correctly ridden shoulder-in increases suppleness and collection through the necessarily active use of the inside hind leg. Once you have developed the feel of the movement you will wonder how you ever managed without it.

As a rider you will have developed the use of independent leg and rein aids and this will greatly enhance your communication with your horse.

TRAVERS

Once you have mastered shoulder-in and your horse is able to do it easily and well, travers is another useful suppling exercise.

Begin the exercise on the long side of the school. The walls give you more control.

Travers.

Your horse must be bent in the direction in which he is going, with his head towards the wall and his quarters towards the inside of the arena. The bend through his body is similar to that in shoulder-in.

First position your horse with a correct bend as you come through the corner. Keep your inside leg on the girth to maintain the bend, and keep your horse moving forwards. Your outside leg behind the girth pushes your horse's quarters towards the inside of the arena. The inside rein should be light, as it asks for the bend to the inside. The outside rein is secure but passive as it maintains the correct amount of bend. The feeling of bending your horse around your inside leg is quite definite. Your weight should be a little more on your inside seat bone. This stops you sliding to the outside of the saddle.

This exercise has to be introduced quite gradually, as it is more difficult for your horse than shoulder-in.

RENVERS

The only difference between renvers and travers is that in renvers your horse has his forehand to the inside and his quarters towards the wall.

Begin exactly as though you were going to do shoulder-in, then gradually change the bend with the same aids as for travers. Be careful to maintain the rhythm and the impulsion.

As with travers, this exercise is quite difficult for your horse at first. Have patience and remember that he will easily become tired.

HALF-PASS

If you are beginning to think: 'Oh no, this is too difficult for me', please don't, because the benefits of these movements to your horse are so great. You will soon discover that the progression through shoulder-in to travers and travers to renvers leads you, without any problems, to half-pass.

In half-pass the horse moves in a forward and sideways manner across the school on the diagonal. He is bent and looking in the direction in which he is travelling.

His outside legs cross in front of his inside legs.

He should maintain the same balance, rhythm and impulsion throughout the whole movement.

He should travel almost parallel to the long side, but though his quarters should not trail behind, his shoulders should be slightly in advance of his quarters.

A good half-pass right except that the rider is leaning the wrong way. Good crossing of the hind legs and correct positioning and bend.

Half-pass is introduced first in trot and afterwards in canter.

The rider first prepares the horse by positioning him either on the track at the beginning of the long side or down the centre line, continuing on the rein he has already been on. The positioning is as for shoulder-in with the shoulders off the track. The inside leg on the girth keeps the impulsion and the bend, while the inside rein gently maintains the bend and the direction. The inside rein must not pull. The outside leg behind the girth pushes the quarters over and the outside rein controls the shoulder and the degree of forward movement.

Most riders tend to neglect the importance of their inside leg and it is all too often seen stuck forward and not in use. Even more important is the placing of the rider's weight on the inside seat bone instead of allowing it to slip to the outside, where it blocks the movement: an all too common occurrence.

In the beginning you must be satisfied with a few steps forward and across. Try to keep a soft bend and maintain the same angle of your horse's body as he travels forward and sideways instead of wobbling from the diagonal line.

Half-pass right with good crossing (LEFT) and half-pass left with good crossing (RIGHT).

Always be content with a little at first. Build up very gradually towards a stronger sideways angle and be ready to return to more forward and less sideways movement if problems emerge.

Never let tension creep into any work with your horse, particularly lateral work. Tension will always be the enemy of suppleness, regularity and real impulsion.

HALF PIROUETTE IN WALK

The half pirouette at walk is a half turn with the horse's forehand making a circle round his inside hind leg.

Your horse should be bent in the direction in which he is turning and should keep the proper four-beat sequence of walk steps. The rhythm of the steps should be maintained and, ideally, his inside hind leg should be lifted and placed down again on the same spot.

It is better to begin half pirouettes using the track and turning inwards so that the wall stops your horse stepping backwards.

To ask for pirouette you must prepare by having an active walk and shortening the steps without slowing the rhythm. Bend your horse as if you were going to begin shoulder-in. Keep your inside leg on the girth and make sure that it maintains the impulsion. The outside leg, behind the girth, holds the quarters and stops them stepping sideways, while the inside rein asks for a soft bend and the outside rein controls the forward movement and helps to bring the shoulder round the hind legs.

Horses do not find walk pirouettes difficult but riders do. They are a little like shoulder-in, in that once you have developed the knack you will find them easy.

In the beginning, don't expect your horse to keep his inside leg on the spot. Instead, make him step a little forward with each step so that his hind legs make a small half circle and his front legs a much bigger one. Gradually you can make the half circle smaller.

COUNTER-CANTER

When your horse is well balanced and able to show a degree of collection in canter you can introduce counter-canter. The easiest way to describe this is to say it is cantering with the wrong leg leading on purpose: i.e. if you are travelling to the right your horse will be leading with his left leg.

The best reason for doing counter-canter is that it helps collection and increases suppleness. The other reason is that it demonstrates your horse's obedience to your aids.

Your horse must be bent in the direction of his leading leg. It is particularly important for the correct three beats of the canter to be maintained, for in the beginning there is a danger that your horse will find this movement uncomfortable and difficult, will lose the suppleness of his back and the spring in his stride and will canter with four beats, which, as you know, is totally incorrect.

Counter-canter may be asked for in the beginning by just riding a shallow loop, then making it deeper, until little by little you can complete a large circle.

As you change direction from canter into counter-canter you must hold your horse in 'the wrong lead' by keeping the inside leg on the

Counter-canter.

girth and the outside leg back. Make sure that the weight stays in the inside seat bone, and keep the bend of the horse to the outside with the usual light contact of the inside rein and the support of the outside rein. *Remember: when I mention 'inside' and 'outside' I am referring to the bend. If the left leg is leading, your horse will be bent to the left* BUT WILL BE CIRCLING TO THE RIGHT.

There are, of course, many more advanced movements, including flying changes, but they are outside the scope of this book. At more advanced levels there is no substitute for correct instruction.

CHAPTER FIFTEEN

A Pattern of Training

To be able to train a horse completely from the beginning requires skill and knowledge. Unless you are already an established and experienced rider you should not attempt to back and train an unbroken horse. Two beginners together can only confuse each other.

In the beginning your horse has to learn how to carry a weight on his back and how to respond to simple, fundamental aids. If the weight he is asked to carry is as unstable as he is, and if the aids are not accurately applied, he will quickly become resentful and confused.

The untrained horse cannot progress beyond the knowledge of his rider, so throughout all your riding life your horse can only be as good as you are able to make him. It is very much easier to learn to ride dressage on a horse that has already been trained by an expert – for he as good as tells you, out loud, when you have given the wrong signals.

In other words, if you are going to train your own horse you have to know a little more than he does. At the same time you also have to keep ahead of him with your own athletic skills.

The pattern of training given below stems from the German system and assumes that the horse has been correctly backed. I am including the list only because I believe it is helpful to have some strong guidelines to refer to when you have difficulties.

I hope that you yourself have not had to be responsible for the early training of your horse – unless you have had a lot of experience or expert advice.

Most of you will have a horse or pony who is in regular work, is safe with traffic and on the roads, and understands the simple aids. Even better, he may also have been jumped and ridden across country, alone and in the company of other horses.

As long as he is not younger than four-and-a-half he should now be strong and mature enough to begin the schooling work that you are going to do together.

It is important to fill in the gaps in his education by going back to the beginning of the training programme. Think of it as a sort of revision.

As soon as you discover a weak link in his way of going or obedience, go back to the previous stage and make certain that there is nothing amiss there. Never be afraid to go back if it means helping your horse to understand.

To be able to advance your horse's training you must have a truly independent seat. This means that you can keep your balance on your horse's back without holding on with your hands or legs. Only when your seat is independent can you use your legs and hands in different ways.

THE HORSE

Stage 1

Work should be principally in trot and walk, but with some canter.

Obedience to your forward aids must be learned and supported by corrections with the schooling whip.

Your horse must understand and obey the aids to slow down and to turn.

He must accept the bit without fuss or resistance.

He should be willing to canter and should have begun to understand the aids to canter on a named leg.

ACHIEVEMENT: Your horse has regained the natural way of going that he had before a rider sat on his back.

Stage 2

Now you can teach a greater understanding of the forward and controlling aids. As his understanding increases, more activity and freedom of the paces can be developed.

You teach him to move more actively forward without hurrying. Increased suppleness will result from his learning to involve his whole body as he moves.

You will feel *when* your horse *is working through his back*, instead of holding himself stiffly, *and will be able to sit to the trot* instead of rise.

Through this more energetic work strengthening his back muscles he will *learn to balance himself. His paces become more regular and springy.*

ACHIEVEMENT: Rhythm.

Stage 3

Your horse can now be expected to step forward into the contact of the rein and work on the bit.

He should work into the outside rein, and any tendency to unequalness should be corrected.

He must be encouraged to use his hind legs actively. Only when a horse is working from his hind legs through a supple poll can his balance and carriage be improved.

ACHIEVEMENT: Your horse can now be ridden correctly on the bit. You should have no difficulty in maintaining this as long as you have never forced the horse into an artificial way of carrying himself. You can ride with a proper rein contact.

Stage 4

As your horse develops more swing through his body you can ask for more impulsion.

Half-halts will be developed.

He must learn to respond actively and willingly to your aids.

More elasticity can be expected in both canter and trot.

The hind quarters propel and push.

ACHIEVEMENT: Lightness of the forehand and a supple back.

Stage 5

A fuller understanding of diagonal and lateral aids is developed.

Lateral work is introduced.

The straightness of your horse must be developed.

You must pay careful attention to his suppleness and ability to bend correctly.

ACHIEVEMENT: Straightness.

Stage 6

Through lateral exercises, counter-canter and direct transitions from canter to walk and walk to canter, the weight-bearing qualities of the hind legs are increased.

ACHIEVEMENT: Collection and extension. The basic schooling work is now completed and your horse is ready to begin advanced work.

THE RIDER

Stage 1

Your position in the saddle must be without major faults – such as crookedness, lack of balance, busy hands or flapping legs.

You must be able to use your hands, arms and legs independently and sit in a balanced way in the centre of the saddle.

You should know and understand the aids and learn the important role your weight and the influence your seat will have on the way in which your horse goes.

You should be able to use a schooling whip correctly.

Stage 2

Through your own increased suppleness, balance and general fitness you should develop a greater feel for the giving of smaller aids. As a result your horse will respond more readily.

You will start to understand the feel of your horse going forward correctly.

You should have learned the correct movement of your body in all paces and be able to ride effectively in sitting trot without causing your horse to cringe away from your seat.

It is important for you to be already able to keep and maintain either a light or a more positive rein contact, as required.

Stage 3

You should know and understand the lateral aids.

You should fully understand what the correct bend is, and should be able to distinguish between a supple and a stiff horse.

You should be aware of the importance of the outside rein in controlling your horse's shoulders.

You should be able to use the seat and weight aids without making them obvious.

Stage 4

You should be able to apply the lateral aids effectively and should generally know how to control the whole body of your horse.

You should have become a rider who is capable of doing, thinking and planning.

Stage 5

You should have acquired enough experience to correct bad habits and to improve most horses.

Stage 6

You begin to realise how much you still have to learn. You will constantly seek further knowledge.

As the two programmes mature together, you and your horse will find that you are enjoying your training times together more and more.

CHAPTER SIXTEEN

Training Exercises

Schooling work should be well planned, have a beginning, a middle and an end, and be constructive.

Unfortunately most people begin their training period in an aimless way, and they tend to meander around the schooling area without thinking positively about what they want to achieve.

Every day should have a basic framework, divided into three phases:

The loosening or warming-up phase.
The working phase.
The unwinding or relaxation phase.

There are no set rules about how long each phase should take. Each horse is an individual.

A horse who is confident about the work he is doing and is therefore relaxed in his mind will take a shorter time than a horse who is worried and uncertain of what his rider is asking him to do.

The horse who is at Stage 1 will spend his whole work period doing loosening work, while the horse who has reached Stage 5 will probable spend ten minutes or even less on this. You do not have to rely on your own judgment of how long you should spend; instead, you must continue until your horse, through the way he goes, tells you he is ready to proceed.

There is no reason why you can't do your loosening-up work by taking a short ride around the fields.

The working phase builds up gradually through suppling exercises which include circles, turns, curved lines, changes of rein, transitions and work over poles.

When these suppling exercises have achieved their objective and your horse is taking a steady contact on the rein you can proceed with exercises of greater difficulty: *but not until you are sure that your horse is working correctly*.

If you introduce more difficult work before your horse is relaxed and supple, progress will be impossible.

During the work period it is essential to return to a few loosening and suppling exercises after some new or testing movements that might cause your horse to lose his inner calmness. Tranquillity must always be restored.

Even during the working phase, care should be taken to return to simple work which your horse thoroughly understands, so that his confidence in you, and in himself, is regained.

The unwinding phase is really a repeat of the first loosening-up phase, but it should be ridden on a long rein and predominantly in walk. A quiet hack down the road can be a pleasant ending to a happy hour.

EXERCISES FOR THE LOOSENING WORK

I personally do not believe that exactly the same work routine should be carried out every day, but the following six exercises suggest a basic pattern:

1. Working on a long rein in walk round the field or school.
2. Walking over poles (set at approximately 1 metre apart. Never walk over poles set at a trotting distance).
3. Trot work with a light contact on large circles or straight lines. Changes of rein can be included.
4. Canter work on big circles and on the straight, perhaps all the way round the field. The rider may take his seat out of the saddle to encourage the horse to use his back.
5. Transitions to and from canter, again on a light contact.
6. Transitions to walk from trot, and to trot again.

At the end of this phase you should have developed rhythm and activity and a swinging back. Your horse should be breathing with a soft blow that partners the rhythm of his steps.

WORKING PHASE

Below is a series of exercises, some with diagrams, which are classically used for developing a well-trained horse up to medium level.

It is important to realise that these exercises must be achieved gradually. You do not suddenly go from riding a 20-metre circle to riding a 10-metre one.

Different ways of changing the rein:

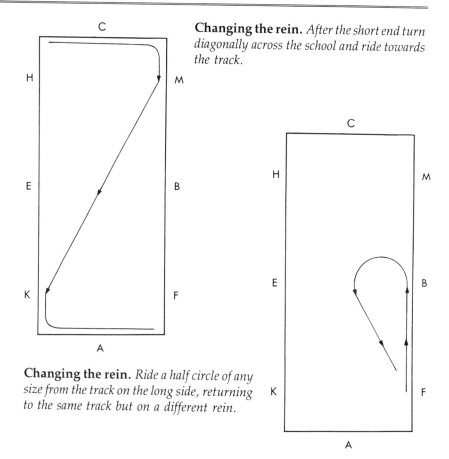

Changing the rein. *After the short end turn diagonally across the school and ride towards the track.*

Changing the rein. *Ride a half circle of any size from the track on the long side, returning to the same track but on a different rein.*

1. On the diagonal. After the short end, turn diagonally across the school and ride towards the track.

2. Two large half circles from A or C. The changes of rein occurs as you cross X.

3. A half circle from the track on the long side, returning back to the same track but on a different rein.

4. Turning down the centre line or directly across the arena. Ride the turn as if it were half a 10-metre circle.

5. A turn on the forehand. This may be asked for anywhere, as long as the horse is not so close to the wall or hedge that he has nowhere to put his head as he begins the turn.

6. A serpentine of two, four, or six loops, begun at A or C. In the beginning the loops of the serpentine should touch the track, they should be of equal size and the horse's change of bend should be made with the change of direction each time the horse crosses the centre line.

7. A half pirouette. In the beginning the turns should be made inwards using the support of the wall to prohibit any stepping backwards. Later they may be ridden anywhere.

All these changes of direction have training value if they are ridden correctly: i.e. by paying attention to the bend and the straightness.

SUPPLING EXERCISES

A suppling exercise is of no value if it is ridden without feeling. The rider must always be aware of the importance of his horse maintaining a supple back, a relaxed jaw, and rhythm.

The horse must go correctly into the outside rein and be bent round the rider's inside leg.

1. Circles of all sizes.
2. Curved lines, such as loops down the long side which come 5 metres off the track opposite either B or E, or serpentines.
3. Leg yielding. This is best done on the diagonal, either from the centre line or from the track.

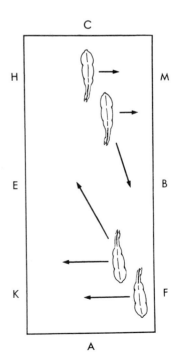

Leg yielding, *shown in two places: (top) travelling from the centre line to the track, where the angle is less acute; (bottom) from the track, where a more acute angle may be ridden.*

4. Turn on the forehand.

5. Changes of rein such as Exercises 2, 3, and 6 of the working phase.

6. Trot circles of approximately 12-14 metres, first on one rein then immediately on the other. Circles may become smaller as training progresses.

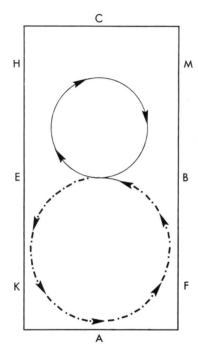

Trot and canter circles. *Circle right in trot approximately 12 metres, then make a transition to canter left at X (dotted line) 20 metres diameter. Trot just before the circle is completed and trot another small circle (continuous line) to the right. Repeat several times without stopping. Repeat on the other rein.*

7. Trot circle, as above, on the right rein then canter left on a 20-metre circle. Trot just before the circle is completed and trot another smaller circle to the right. Repeat on the other rein.

8. Spiral inwards from a 20-metre circle, gradually reducing to a 10-metre circle and back out again.

9. Shoulder-in on the straight.

10. Shoulder-in on the circle.

11. Travers on the straight.

12. Travers on the circle.

13. Shoulder-in on the straight, changing to travers, and returning to shoulder-in.

All work should be in trot unless I have specifically mentioned another pace.

EXERCISES FOR DEVELOPING MORE ENGAGEMENT OF THE HIND QUARTERS

1. All transitions, with particular attention to trot-walk-trot. It often helps to begin these on a circle.

2. Transitions to halt from trot and from halt into trot. Again, these can be easier on a circle.

3. Transitions from walk to a few strides of canter followed by a transition, progressive at first, back to walk. Guard the walk carefully, as this exercise can create tension and irregularities of pace if overdone. To begin with, it is much easier on a curved line.

4. The half-halt – used as a preparation to all movements.

5. Shoulder-in and travers on the straight and also on a circle.

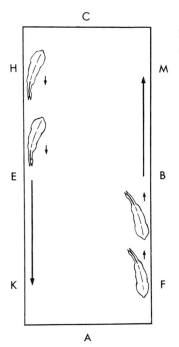

Shoulder-in and travers (quarters-in). *Shoulder-in F-M followed by travers H-K.*

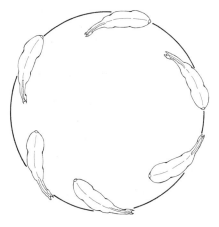

Shoulder-in and travers on the circle. *At the top the horse's shoulders are brought in off the track of the circle, then at the bottom the horse's quarters are brought in off the track of the circle.*

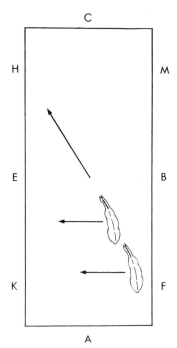

Half-pass left.

6. Half-pass.

7. Counter-canter. The first introduction should be made by riding a shallow loop. Later ride a half circle of not more than 10 metres towards the end of the long side returning to the track at approximately the half marker and making a transition to trot before the corner. Finally the horse is kept in counter-canter through a 'soft' corner (the edges taken off) or on a big circle anywhere. The size of the circle is gradually decreased until 10 metres is achieved at Prix St George level.

8. Half pirouettes in walk.

9. Collected trot-medium trot-collected trot. At first only a few steps of medium trot should be allowed so that the balance is maintained. This exercise can be carried out at any point in the arena, or on the diagonal with collected trot to X and medium trot afterwards. The value of the exercise lies in the transitions.

10. Collected walk should *not* be asked for until your horse has a well-developed collected trot and canter. Even then it should be practised very little. Suppling exercises, such as shoulder-in and leg yielding on a circle are the best introduction to collected walk.

11. Voltes (circles of 6 metres diameter) can be ridden anywhere and used to correct a lack of bend as well as being an overall suppling exercise. They should be used only with advanced horses, and even then are of no value unless the horse remains in balance, keeps his rhythm, and has his hind legs following his front legs.

Flying changes, canter pirouettes, piaffe and passage are more advanced movements that will further develop the horse's balance and collection.

Conclusion

If you read these notes carefully you will realise that all the movements ridden in dresage tests and training help to improve paces, suppleness and collection. Riding a horse that has good paces, impulsion, suppleness, balance and obedience is sheer delight. It is what dressage training is all about. The prime aim is to produce the perfect riding horse, *not* to win prizes because you can do piaffe better than anyone else!

CHAPTER SEVENTEEN

Understanding a Dressage Test

When you decide to enter a competition, the schedule will tell you which test you have to ride. Make sure that you learn the right one!

Test sheets can generally be bought through your Pony Club branch or national equestrian organisation.

In less difficult tests the arena is 40 metres × 20 metres. At higher levels the arena is usually longer and measures 60 metres × 20 metres.

Look at the diagrams and study the letters around the outside. The large arena has four more letters than the smaller one. Competition arenas are marked out by boards, rope or a white line. The outside letters are shown in black on white, but the centre line and the inside letters marking it are indicated by mown strips of grass. The entrance to the arena is at A. The judge sits at C. Sometimes there is more than one judge, but for young riders never more than three, except at championship level. In very advanced competitions for adults there are sometimes as many as five judges.

When you read your first test it may seem difficult to understand and impossible to learn. But don't panic! Your first test really will be quite simple to understand as long as you carefully follow what it says.

Reading through the test sheet you will see that it is actually a list of movements with numbers down the left-hand side. Each number represents a particular *movement*. Learn the test one movement at a time.

Until you are experienced it is easier to understand exactly where you have to ride by drawing out each movement on pieces of paper. Draw an oblong and put the letters round it. You will need a separate drawing for each movement.

The first movement will probably say something like:

1.A Enter at working trot.
  X Halt, salute and proceed in working trot.
  C Track right.

This is an easy movement to draw: a line from A straight down the centre line with a mark at X to tell you where to halt. At C let your line curve to the right on the sort of track you will be able to ride round the corner and stop at M. *The movement always ends at the marker where the next movement begins.*

The next movement could say:

2. M – B   Working trot.
   B   Circle right 20 metres diameter.
   B   Working trot.

Look at the diagram which shows you how the arena is divided up mathematically and you will realise that a 20-metre circle has to touch the far side of the arena and come 10 metres from each end. Draw it on your next diagram and you will see what I mean. Look ahead to Movement 3 and see at which letter it begins. That is where your pencil mark will end for Movement 2.

Unless the test says otherwise, you are expected to stay on the track. Even if some of the letters are missed out *you still go round the track until you get to them.*

When you look at the whole test in diagrams you will generally see a kind of repeat pattern that is not too hard to learn. Some people find it easier to use coloured pencils for different paces.

There are a few rules that will help you understand how to interpret each new test. I have already explained the first one:

1. Stay on the track travelling in the same direction unless you are told to do otherwise.
2. When asked to circle from a marker, ride a circle of the correct size *and return to the same marker at the end of the circle.*
3. When you are told to turn right or left, leave the track just before the marker so that you stay on a line that runs 90° from that marker. Make the turn so that it is a soft corner, like a small half circle.
4. When you are told to 'track right' or 'left' make the same soft turn as you reach the track.
5. Changes of pace when asked for at a marker should be ridden so that the new pace occurs as the rider's body passes the marker. If the transition is progressive (say from walk through trot to canter) it is then the canter which is the new pace, so the transitions must be finished by the time that the rider's body passes the marker. The same applies to downward transitions.

In Great Britain all transitions may be progressive up to and including Elementary standard, *unless it says on the sheet that they may not be.* If this is the case it will say they must be 'direct'.

Rules governing the riding of tests do vary. However, there is one golden rule that remains unchanged: READ THE CURRENT RULE BOOK CAREFULLY.

RIDING THE TESTS

When you start learning to ride the test, try to practise it in small sections, otherwise your horse is going to anticipate the movements.

All the things you have practised at home sometimes get forgotten when you ride into the arena. Only practice will teach you to stay calm and to remember to think ahead. If your first test is a muddle, you have proved yourself to be exactly like most other people. During my first year in dressage I went wrong in every single test. It wasn't that I hadn't learned them. It was just nerves that made me forget.

The most common mistake that most riders make at first is to forget to ride forwards, with the result that lines are wobbly and circles look egg-shaped. Transitions are never correct if your horse isn't going forwards.

Another mistake is trying too hard in the arena, so that your horse wonders what is happening and becomes anxious.

If you do make an error of course, the judge will sound his horn or bell. Stay in the arena and ask the judge where you have gone wrong. *Don't start again until you are quite sure that you know where to go.* You must go back to the beginning of the movement where you made your mistake. It is sensible to go back at least two or three markers so that your horse will be going forward properly before you start to be judged again. Remember, if you do go wrong it is not the end of the world – only two marks off the total, in fact!

Below is a normal Pony Club test that shows you how each movement should be ridden and how the rider should be thinking.

1. A   Enter in working trot
X   Halt, salute, proceed in working trot

Coming out of a circle before you enter, line yourself up well with A so that you can see a clear line down the centre of the arena. A clear run will help to ensure a good halt.

The halt and the transitions into and out of the halt are the most important parts of the movement. Be sure that the trot before the halt is forward, straight and rhythmic.

Prepare for the halt a few strides before X, remembering the 'seat and legs, not hands' rule. Your horse may take two or three strides of walk before he halts, as long as the steps are not 'shuffles'.

The most important point about the halt is that it should be still and

Movement 1

A   Enter in working trot
X   Halt, salute, proceed in working trot

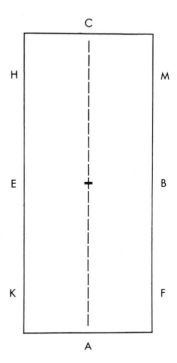

calm. Your horse should be straight, if you have made a good entry. The judge will also be hoping to see a square halt with each of the four legs placed like the corners of a rectangle.

For the salute, take the reins (and stick if permitted and/or carried) into the left hand (in Great Britain they can be taken into either hand) and place the free hand down as if hanging loosely. Ladies bow their heads to the judge at C before retaking the reins. Men remove their hats, holding them briefly down to their sides before replacing them. If wearing a hat with a chin strap, they may salute without removing it. During this salute only the head should be bent forward. The rider should not attempt to bow from the waist.

Your horse must learn to stand quietly and wait for you to give the aids to go forward again when you are ready. The whole salute should take about 10 seconds.

The move-off may be through a few steps of walk into trot and must be ridden positively forward.

Approaching C begin the turn so that the turn and the following corner can be ridden like a half circle. Make sure that you bend your horse correctly before the corner begins.

Most Novice tests may be ridden in sitting or rising trot. Great Britain allows a choice; other countries state on their test sheets which should be ridden.

> REMEMBER: **_Get straight. Ride smooth transitions. A still, square halt._**

2. C   Track right
MBF   Working trot

Ride accurately into the corner with the correct bend. Don't cut the corner.

Ride forward and establish a good swinging rhythm, but don't push your horse out of his balance.

Make a small half-halt before the corner after F and ask for the bend just before the corner. Try to think ahead to the next movement.

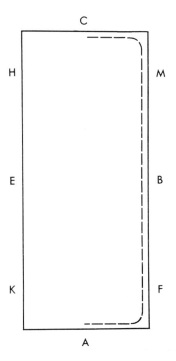

Movement 2

C   *Track right*
MBF *Working trot*

> REMEMBER: **_Forward and rhythmic. Straight. Balanced and bent through the corners._**

3. A-C   Serpentine 3 loops, each loop going to the side of the arena

A serpentine can be ridden in two ways. Either like three half circles joined across the centre with straight lines, or by riding slightly larger half circles and then coming back a little on your track as you cross the arena, thus emphasising the flowing change of rein. In both cases it is most important for the loops to be of equal size.

This is a real test of your horse's suppleness. He must bend equally in both directions, and keep his rhythm and impulsion.

Movement 3

A-C   Serpentine 3 loops, each loop going to the side of the arena

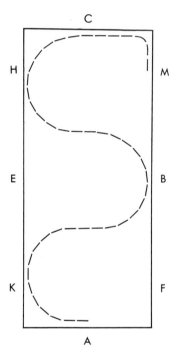

REMEMBER: *The changes of bend. Balance and rhythm. The shape of the loops. Activity.*

4. M   Working canter right
B   Circle right 15 metre diameter

You must be sure to make a small half-halt before the transition to canter. If your horse has been correctly bent throughout the last

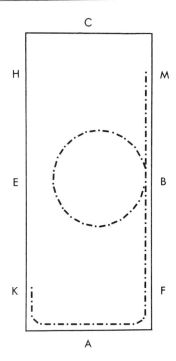

C

H   M

E   B

K   F

A

Movement 4

M   Working canter right
B   Circle right 15 metres diameter

loop of the serpentine he should be well positioned for the strike-off.

Ask for the canter a stride before the marker so that your horse will begin the canter just as your body passes the marker. Keep your horse well into the outside rein to stop his shoulders falling out and his whole body becoming crooked.

Position him with a little more bend as you approach B and look well ahead on the line where you are going to ride your circle. A 15-metre circle will come 5 metres short of E. Make sure that you don't have too much bend in the neck to the inside, or your horse may slide out of the circle on to his outside shoulder. Alternatively, be careful that you have sufficient bend and really have him round your inside leg, otherwise he may put too much weight on his inside shoulder and fall inwards.

As you get back to B straighten him, but don't let him fall on his outside shoulder and become crooked. Use the two following corners to get him really well balanced for the next movement.

REMEMBER: **Ride a well-prepared transition. Keep the rhythm, balance and correct bend. Make sure the circle is the right shape.**

5. KH   One loop 5 metres in from the track

The second part of this loop is really a little bit of counter-canter. Come off the track a fraction before K and keep the bend over the right leg, but have your outside leg firmly behind the girth. As you arrive opposite E begin to take your horse back to the track, *keeping the right bend* by a combination of your inside leg and inside rein, always keeping the outside rein contact. Try to reach the track just before the H marker. Make sure that you keep the impulsion in the canter, otherwise you may lose the rhythm or even the correct sequence of steps. The next two corners are very important, as they are a real help in getting your horse together again after the loop before you have to make the transition to trot.

Movement 5

KH   One loop 5 metres in from the track

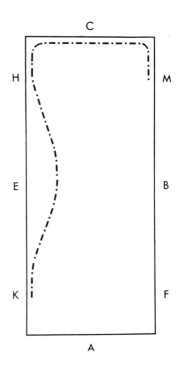

REMEMBER: ***Keep the right bend throughout. Impulsion and rhythm.***

6. MXK   Change the rein
X   Working trot

Make a good half-halt just before the M corner and then leave the M marker so that your horse's shoulders come off the track at that point. Use your seat and legs to prepare for the transition at X and then ride forward so that you immediately find the rhythm of your trot.

Ride to a point about a metre before the K marker and you will find you can then manage to prepare and ride the corner well.

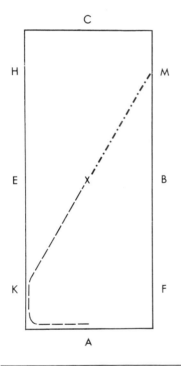

Movement 6
MXK   Change the rein
X   Working trot

REMEMBER: **Prepare by using the corners. Use your seat and legs to make a good transition.**

7. A   Halt, immobility 5 seconds
Proceed in medium walk

The corner you have just ridden is very important. If you have let your horse lose his balance you are going to find it difficult to get him re-balanced before the halt. Ride with your seat and legs, and the least possible rein aids, into the halt. He should stay still and square. It is better to be not quite four-square than to start fidgeting, which spoils everything.

You have to stay still for 5 seconds. Count to yourself: 'one thousand and one, one thousand and two, one thousand and three', and so on. Try to keep a light steady contact throughout the halt so that you can move off smoothly into the medium walk without resistance.

In walk, ride forward but don't hurry your horse.

Movement 7

A   Halt, immobility 5 seconds
Proceed in medium walk

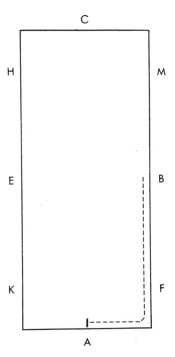

REMEMBER: *A still halt. Good transitions and a regular walk.*

8. B   Half circle left 5 metres diameter returning to the track before F

As you approach B ask for a little more bend to the inside with the fingers. Keep your inside leg firmly on the girth, and as you begin to come off the track at B, make sure your outside leg is behind the girth, holding the quarters. Your outside rein will be very important to stop the shoulders falling out. Try to bend your horse round your inside leg rather than only bend his neck. His steps should remain a clear four beat. Keep his walk purposeful.

As you complete the *half* circle, straighten your horse and head back for the track at a point just before F, changing the bend as you do so. The change of bend is important, as you have to ride through the next two corners on a long rein.

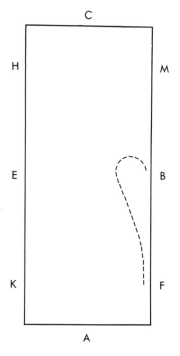

Movement 8

B   Half circle left 5 metres diameter returning to the track before F

REMEMBER: *A regular, purposeful walk, the hind feet following the tracks of the forefeet.*

9. F   Free walk on a long rein
K   Medium walk

As you turn the corner, ride forward and let your horse draw the reins through your hands as he stretches his neck. You want him to keep the same rhythm in his walk and to lengthen his strides a little. He should not snatch the reins but simply stretch his neck forward and down. Sit calmly, and as you come through the second corner, take up the reins again so that your horse is back on the bit by the time you get to K. Be sensitive as you re-take the reins and don't forget to use your legs softly as he feels the rein contact.

Movement 9

F   Free walk on a long rein
K   Medium walk

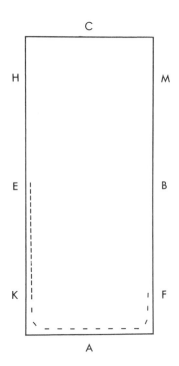

REMEMBER: *Regular but longer steps. No resistance through the transitions. An overall lengthening of the horse's outline.*

The next movement is a repeat of the movement already ridden on the other rein. Can you recognise it?

10. E   Half circle right 5 metres in diameter, returning to the track before F

Instead of letting your horse relax and stretch his neck at the end of the movement you have to make sure that he is paying attention to you.

11. A   Working canter left (directly from walk)
B   Circle left 15 metres diameter

Nearly the same movement as before, but this time you have to make the transition from walk directly into canter – which is not as difficult as it sounds. Make sure that you have the correct bend and that your horse is really active. Don't drop the rein contact, or he is bound to trot. Give the canter aids and *expect to canter*. You will! Then the movement should be just the same as 4.

12. HK   One loop 5 metres in from the track

13. A   Working trot
F   Circle left 10 metres diameter

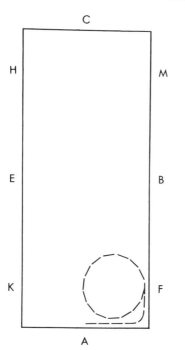

Movement 13
A   Working trot
F   Circle left 10 metres diameter

Though this may seem a rather small circle, and therefore difficult, it is really quite useful in helping you to get your horse well engaged before you ride the next movement. Making a 10-metre circle is very similar to turning down the centre line. That is, after all, half a 10-metre circle. Don't try to pull your horse round with the reins. Ride round using a light inside rein supported by a stronger outside rein to stop the shoulder sliding out. Your outside leg behind the girth will keep the quarters in position and your inside leg on the girth will make the bend and keep the impulsion. Try to keep the trot regular.

REMEMBER: *The transition to trot. The balance, bend and regularity. The shape of the circle.*

---

14. FXH   Change the rein and show a few lengthened strides

If you have ridden the circle correctly it will have helped you to get your horse's hind legs well underneath him and ready to propel him forward into longer steps.

Movement 14
FXH   Change the rein and show a few lengthened strides

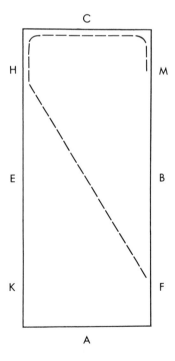

Just before you come off the track at F, make a half-halt. Build the impulsion and let your horse stretch his neck as his steps get longer, but do not lighten the contact; if you do, he will hurry. There should be no change in tempo and the trot must stay regular. Make sure that he doesn't fall on his forehand.

The transition must be smooth and fluent, so that after a few steps of lengthening you are able to return to your working trot just as smoothly. Don't try to ride medium trot from marker to marker. It is not necessary. The transitions into and out of the longer strides are as important as the lengthening.

REMEMBER: **Rhythm. Steady transitions. Balance.**

---

15. M   Circle right 10 metres diameter

Ride as movement 13 but on the opposite rein.

16. MXK   Change rein and show a few lengthened strides

As movement 14.

17. A   Turn down centre line
X   Medium walk
G   Halt, salute
Leave the arena at walk on a long rein at A

You really have to prepare this last movement at K while you are still in the previous movement.

You will have to use quite a lot of seat and leg to rebalance your horse after the lengthening. Prepare for the corner by positioning him with the correct bend. Ride the corner and the turn on to the centre line as for half a 10-metre circle.

Ride forward down the centre line just as you did at the beginning. Use your seat more than your hands to make the transition to walk, and then come through an active, medium walk into the final halt and salute.

See if you can manage a big smile for the judge.

Now you may give your horse the full freedom of his head and neck and leave the arena calmly at A.

Movement 17

A   *Turn down centre line*
X   *Medium walk*
G   *Halt, salute*
     Leave the arena at walk on a long rein
     at A

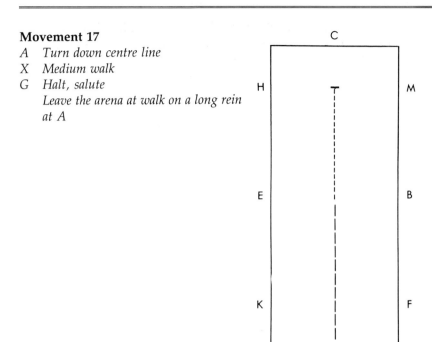

Well done!

CHAPTER EIGHTEEN

The Competition

Try not to think of a competition as something you have been working towards for so many months. Instead, try to think of it as a measurement of how successful you have been at home in your training. Any test in a competition can only prove that you have reached another step on the ladder to having a well-trained horse.

Obviously you will have prepared your horse carefully during the weeks before the competition, making sure that he understands and can do the sort of movements which will be required in the test. Learn thoroughly the tests you are to ride – but don't actually ride through them more than a few times, or your horse will start to anticipate what you are going to ask him to do next. Horses learn very quickly!

Before filling in your entry form be sure to read the schedule carefully. Only enter one or two competitions, having made sure that you and your horse are eligible. Try to write clearly, and post your entries in good time.

Local dressage competitions are often quite small and are not at all frightening.

You will probably be given a number and time to telephone for your starting times. Unlike show jumping, where you have the overall time of the class, in dressage you are given a precise time and *you have to be there and ready to compete or you will be eliminated*. If you have entered two classes, you will be given two times. Don't forget to telephone and ask for these times. The schedule will tell you when to call (it is usually two evenings before the competition).

Write yourself a check-list of all the items that you need to take with you. This is mine:

For the horse

Complete saddle, with numnah
Bridle, complete
Bridle number
Lungeing equipment with two lunge lines
Boots, for riding-in
Studs
Grooming kit
Extra tail bandage and a set of stable bandages with Gamgee
Fly repellent
Hoof oil
Tack-cleaning equipment
Tools for removing a shoe
Veterinary chest
Spare parts chest (spare rein, girth, stirrup leathers and a leather punch, plus pieces of string, needles and strong thread)
Skip
Shovel
Fork
Sweeping brush
Feeds, labelled
Hay net
Water
Buckets (3)
Cooling sheet and lightweight rug
Waterproof sheet
Blanket
Horse passport or vaccination certificate

For the rider

Boots
Spare pair of breeches

Jacket
Two clean stocks or a tie
Safety pins (various sizes)
Stock pin
Hat
Hairnet
Gloves
Whip
Spurs
Raincoat and warm coat
Pair of old loose trousers to wear over breeches
Test book
Rule book
Schedule
Map
Picnic
Money
Bootjack
Folding chair
Carrots (for horse!)

My horse travels in leg protectors, hock boots, knee pads, tail bandage and tail guard, suitable rugs depending on the weather (roller if necessary), and a headcollar with a rope attached.

I take lungeing tack, though I seldom use it. (You can use two ropes if you or someone else has a horse who won't load.)

Prepare your lorry or trailer the day before and load as much as you can the night before.

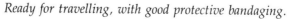

Ready for travelling, with good protective bandaging.

A quick, modern alternative to bandaging are these snap-on travelling boots.

Check the stud holes in your horse's shoes and pack them with twists of cotton-wool for easy removal.

Groom thoroughly, and do any last-minute trimming. Skip out the stable as late as possible at night then there will be less chance of a stained horse next morning.

Though plaiting may be done the night before, I always think it must be rather uncomfortable for the horse, so generally I try to do it in the morning. (Don't forget to put the plaiting equipment in your grooming box, including the scissors.)

Try to arrive at the show *at least* two hours before your first dressage time. On arrival, check your horse and, depending on the weather, open up your box or trailer. Go to the Secretary's tent as soon as possible. Buy a programme, ask for your number, and find out the lay of the land.

It is quite a good idea to go over to the arena area and ask the steward how the class is progressing. If it is running behind it may mean that your time will be later.

If your horse is inexperienced it is a good plan to take him out of the box early, and I do recommend putting on a lungeing cavesson to give you more control if he becomes very excited.

Walk him round and let him see the sights. As long as he is calm and unworried, that's fine, but if he fails to settle it might be a good idea to tack up and ride him round. Very often when a horse is excited, the first time that he is taken out of the box he settles quickly if he is put away and then brought out again later. I always do this with a young horse. They seem to accept the party atmosphere much better the second time out.

Quite a lot of riders like to have studs in their horses' shoes. This can be a big help on grass if the going is other than perfect, and they can be screwed in after unloading. You need two kinds: small sharp ones for hard, slippery ground, and big, square ones for skiddy mud or wet grass.

Before you leave your box, make sure to arrange everything tidily. Put any valuable items out of sight or preferably lock them up. Ask a friend or helper to take your jacket, clothes brush, grooming equipment and fly repellent to the warming-up area.

Ask a friend or helper to take the things you'll need at the last minute – e.g. jacket and grooming kit – to the working-in area.

Remember that you must not ride-in using any piece of saddlery that is not allowed in the dressage arena, except boots and bandages.

Don't forget to put your hat and number on.

For your real 'riding-in' leave about forty minutes plus five minutes extra for a final tidy–up for both of you.

Well turned out and ready to compete.

Check again with the stewards on the timing. They will be grateful to know that you are there anyway.

Ride-in with consideration for other people. If you are riding-in in an arena, pass left hand to left hand. If you are in walk, keep off the track. Give way to riders doing lateral work, flying changes or extensions. Don't ride too close to other horses' hind legs.

Follow the pattern of working-in that you normally use. Don't fall into the trap of trying to do things that will impress other competitors. Remember to allow periods of rest.

It is quite a good idea to identify the two competitors who will ride their tests immediately before you. You can keep an eye on them and be absolutely ready when your time comes.

It is sensible to arrive at your arena as soon as the competitor before you has finished. This gives you extra time to get your horse used to the boards and to the judge's car or box.

Trot calmly round on both reins and make a halt as you ride towards the judge's car. This gives your horse a chance to look over the hedge and see what's there before you actually arrive in the arena. Weave in and out of the markers, too, *but don't make an issue of anything.* If your horse shies at flower pots let him go round them and just give him a pat. *Don't* force him up to them.

Check your riding time with the steward.

Listen for the judge's signal (horn, bell or whistle) and then prepare carefully and make a calm entry. You have sixty seconds in which to enter the arena, which is quite a long time.

If you start off by making a bad turn and presenting yourself awkwardly at the entrance, turn away and approach again.

You may be feeling nervous. Most people do. Try to think of three things:

1. Your own position and how your body feels.
2. Your horse and how he is feeling.
3. The test.

If you really concentrate, there isn't any time for nerves. Anyway, what is there to be nervous about? Judges generally judge because they like to help and encourage riders and horses. Try to be honest with yourself and realise that you are only nervous because you want to do well.

As a last resort, if you feel very tense breathe *out* – yes, *out* – very slowly. The air always comes back into your lungs but really emptying them is far better than deep breaths in, which I find only make me feel tense.

Nearly always in a test something happens that could have been avoided. These are what I call '*if only*' mistakes. You generally blame yourself for them: probably rightly so.

If you go wrong, it isn't the end of the world. Stay calm, don't leave the arena, but ask the judge what you should have done. Before you re-start the test, make sure that you are really clear in you mind. You have only lost two marks anyway.

In some tests it is possible to miss out a whole movement, such as a circle. Very occasionally the judge fails to notice your error, in which case ride on unless he rings the bell. But if you leave out something, like a change of rein, it is better to stop and explain, otherwise you will finish the test going down the arena and saluting with your back to the judge. This sort of thing seldom happens – but judges are only human. (You may not quite believe this, but it's true!)

Simpler things that go wrong are sometimes the horse's fault. If he halts in a very crooked way or won't stand still for even a second, don't go on endlessly trying to make a correction. It only underlines your problem. If, however, you strike off on the wrong leg you *must* keep trying to correct it. If you show no canter on the named leg you will receive a zero mark for the movement. If you show some of the correct canter you will certainly be given some marks. The judge is entitled to give you zero for any movement which is not performed: so, if you jog throughout a walk movement that will be zero!

Do not dismount in the arena unless instructed to do so by the judge.

Do not leave the arena until the end of the test, and then only through the entrance at A.

All these facts are in the rule books, which I know are rather boring to read. However, do try to make yourself sit down at the beginning of each season and just see what has changed.

When the test is over, dismount and reward the horse. If something has gone very wrong and he has really misunderstood what you have asked, go quietly away and try to relax him and sort the problem out. Don't take your disappointment out on the horse with useless punishment. It will do lasting harm to you both.

After you have put the horse away and made him comfortable you can go and look at your score. In pure dressage the highest score is best. In horse trials dressage, the score is converted into penalty points, so the lowest score is the best. When you see your mark, work out how you have gone by your placing in relationship to other competitors. Every test has a different number of movements that add up to a different total, and also judges do not always score on the same scale. Don't be depressed, therefore, if your mark is lower than on a previous occasion (or too happy because it is higher).

At the end of the class you will be able to collect your score sheet with the judge's marks and comments on it. This is always valuable and you should read particularly carefully the final marks for: Paces; Impulsion; Submission; and Rider.

Try not to be nervous, breathe out, concentrate on your pony and enjoy dressage competitions, like this young rider does. Good luck!

Only in these final marks does the judge really have time to write down what he considers are your good and weak points. Take his or her comments to heart for they will be well-considered opinions.

Learn by your mistakes.

CHAPTER NINETEEN

What the Judge Said

The first thing you are going to do when you receive your completed test sheet after a competition is to study the marks. They are very important indeed, and as you look at them remember what the scale of marks means.

10. Excellent
9. Very good
8. Good
7. Fairly good
6. Satisfactory
5. Sufficient
4. Insufficient
3. Fairly bad
2. Bad
1. Very bad
0. Not performed

Translate the marks into the words and your whole sheet should make more sense.

Look particularly at the 'end marks' where there are generally 3×10 marks for the way in which the horse has gone and 1×10 for the rider. This is where you can really assess where your problems lie.

My daughter in her Pony Club days used to look and see whether she had a better or worse mark than her pony. She liked beating him! Seriously, it is quite important to know whether the judge thought that the mistakes were your fault. If he did, your mark will be lower than your horse's.

The first of these end-marks is for *paces*. If your horse has three good paces which haven't been spoiled, you could well get a high mark here, even if you made dozens of mistakes. If one pace is faulty – such as an irregular walk or a four-beat canter, you will be lucky to be given more than a 5.

The next mark is for *impulsion*. This includes suppleness of the back and engagement of the quarters, as well as general activity. A good mark here means that your training is going well.

The final mark for your horse is for *submission*. This means obedience without resistance, lightness and ease of movements, and acceptance of the bridle. You could be given a bad mark here if your horse was inattentive or naughty even though he was basically going well. Equally, it is quite possible to get a good mark even if there are some flaws in your basic training.

You have to really consider these marks carefully and try to understand what your basic faults are. Ask yourself the questions:

Paces

Is the mark not good because the paces are naturally not good, or is there something wrong which I might be able to improve, like a lack of freedom or regularity?

Impulsion

Has he stiffened his back because of the way I have ridden him? Is he lacking impulsion because I have not encouraged forward movement? Is he stiff because I have not made him supple? Is he too much on his forehand for his level of training?

Submission

Does he fuss with his head because my hands are fixed or rough or because his mouth hurts? Is he disobedient because I am not clear and he has not understood? Is there no harmony between us because he has not learned to trust me? Does he lack lightness because I allow him to lean on my hands.?

Rider's mark

It is perhaps rather difficult to ask questions about yourself, especially if you have honestly asked yourself the ones I have suggested above. Don't expect the judge to give you a riding lesson. All he is expected to do is mention things he can actually *see* that you do wrong. Pay attention if he says you are sitting crookedly or have fixed your arms.

Throughout the sheet the judge will have been making comments in a sort of 'dressage shorthand'. At first this may be a bit difficult to understand.

ABOVE BIT – Nose stuck out and back hollow.

AMBLE – A two-beat walk.

BASE WIDE – Hind and forelegs too spread out, not sufficiently under the horse (halting like a hackney).

BEHIND BIT – Dropping the bit.

BROKEN-NECKED – Nose behind vertical. Neck bent at third vertebra more than in the rest of the neck.

BROKEN RHYTHM – The rhythm (of the the walk) 1-2 ... 3-4.

CROOKED – Any deviation of the quarters or forehand resulting in the hind legs not following the forelegs. When referring to the rider it means not sitting absolutely square.

CROUP HIGH – Croup higher than withers, usually inferring that the horse is not bending the joints of his hind legs.

DISUNITED – Cantering with different leads of fore and hind legs.

EARTHBOUND – Lacking spring and elasticity. Lacking suspension. Can be applied to trot or canter.

FALLING IN – The horse puts more weight on his inside shoulder than the outside, with the result that he leans and travels inwards on a circle, often with the wrong bend.

FALLING OUT – The opposite to the above. Often caused by too much bend in the neck and not enough contact of the outside rein.

FELL INTO. . . – Usually applied to a transition down when the horse loses balance and falls heavily on to his forehand.

GOING SHORT – Meaning 'irregular' as below.

GRINDING – Grinding teeth.

IRREGULAR – Steps (generally in walk, trot or rein-back) not regular. Can be either less weight being put on one leg or the range of movement of a leg being reduced in relationship to its pair.

LACKS SUSPENSION – Lacking spring.

LAME – This term is seldom used in dressage without the horse being eliminated.

LEANING – The rider having a lot of weight in his hands due to the horse leaning down on to the bit.

LOSING RHYTHM – Not keeping an absolutely regular beat. It can apply to any pace.

MUDDLED TRANS – Trans is an abbreviation for transition. Muddled transition means that the preceding steps into the new pace were not absolutely in sequence.

NOT □ – Shorthand for 'not square' (as in halt).

NOT DIRECT – Some steps of an unasked-for pace have been included, for example instead of halt-trot some walk steps have been included.

NOT ENGAGED – The horse's hind legs not being placed far enough under his body.

NOT EXPANDING FRAME – The whole outline of the horse not lengthening.

NOT SQUARE – Horse not standing with his hooves forming a rectangle.

NOT ROUND – Shorthand for 'circle not round'.

ON FOREHAND – The horse's hind legs are not correctly underneath him, so there is too much weight on his forehand.

OUT OF SEQ. – Shorthand for the steps of the pace not being in correct sequence.

OVERBENT – The horse bends his neck in such a way that his poll is lower than his crest and his nose is behind the vertical.

Q. IN – Shorthand for quarters in.

RES. – Shorthand for resisting.

RUNNING – Hurried, quick steps. The horse just using his legs instead of working through his whole body.

SHORT BEHIND – Irregular steps with one hind leg.

SHORTENING NECK – Drawing neck back in a tense way.

SHUFFLED – Unclear steps, possibly out of the correct sequence of the pace. It could be used about a poor rein-back.

SNATCHING – Snatching at the rein.

STIFF HOCKS – Hocks not bending.

STUCK – One or all legs of the horse becomes stationary when it/they should be moving.

TIGHT – The horse is holding himself in a tense way in some part of his body.

TILTING – The head tipping sideways.

TIPPING – As above.

TONGUE – Shorthand for the horse's tongue hanging out.

TOO BIG – Applied to a circle or pirouette which is too large.

TOO DEEP – The horse, though remaining on the bit, lowers his head and neck and brings his nose behind the vertical.

TRAILING – Can be applied to the horse that does not have his hind legs underneath him enough, or to the half-pass when the quarters fail to keep in line with the shoulder but are left behind.

TRANS – Shorthand for transition.

TWO-BEAT WALK – An incorrect walk when the near fore and hind legs make one stride together and the off fore and hind make the second stride together.

UNBALANCED – Usually when the horse keeps losing rhythm through not having his hind legs consistently far enough underneath him. It can happen when the horse lacks impulsion and fails to sustain the rhythm because of it.

UNLEVEL – The nearest a dressage judge will get to saying your horse is lame without eliminating you.

WANDERING – Not keeping a straight line.

WIDE – Usually used about the hind legs in either halt or extended trot when the horse has his hind legs unnaturally wide apart. It is a sign of a lack of balance.

WIDE BEHIND – As above.

I'm sure that I have missed out quite a few other comments. All judges tend to use their own type of remark.

I hope that after all your careful schooling there are lots of blank spaces where the comments normally go on your sheet. High numbers by the empty spaces will tell you all that you need to know. Judges seldom write comments if the mark is a 7 or higher!

If you haven't time to wait for your sheet at the end of a class, leave a stamped addressed envelope and the Secretary will post it on to you.

It's quite fun to keep them. One day it will be interesting to look back.

CHAPTER TWENTY

Organisations That Help

There is a worldwide network of organisations involved in the administration of dressage. Foremost is the International Equestrian Federation or Fédération Equestre Internationale, which governs all competing equestrian disciplines. All countries belonging to this organisation generally base their national rules and tests on its principles. This huge organisation is known as the FEI.

Every country in the world that competes internationally in equestrian events is a member of the FEI for it is responsible for the conduct of all international competitions.

Member countries have their own federations, although sometimes it may be called a society or an association.

These societies all have individual members. They have committees that organise the separate disciplines (dressage, show jumping, eventing, driving, etc.). They register horses, keep records of winnings, make national rules, organise competitions and generally look after everything to do with horses in their own country. If you own a horse or a pony you really have a duty, whether you compete or not, to be a member of your national federation, society or association.

In Great Britain, the British Horse Society not only organises all the competitive side of things, but also looks after the welfare of horses, safety laws, keeps bridle paths open, and does a hundred and one other things for the good of those who ride.

The American Horse Shows Association does similar work, as does the Canadian Equestrian Federation, the Equestrian Federation of Australia, and of Ireland, and the New Zealand Horse Society Incorporated.

It is to these organisations that you should write to find out how to become a member and whether they have a separate dressage organisation. They will also tell you of any youth organisations that exist that are involved with dressage.

All the above countries have competitions for young riders and some send teams to international competitions.

In many countries throughout the world there is also the Pony Club, a youth organisation that is worldwide.

They generally have a network of 'branches' throughout the country. This means that you probably have a branch in your area. Throughout the year they have rallies, competitions and all sorts of social get-togethers.

Here is a list of some of the English-speaking national federations and Pony Clubs that you can write to for further information:

Australia
Equestrian Federation of
Australia Inc.
77, King William Rd
North Adelaide
South Australia 5006

The Australian Pony Club
Council Incorporated
Sec. Mrs. R. Brideoak
P.O.Box 46
Lockhart
New South Wales 2656
(This Pony Club is divided into 8
states with a total of 905
branches.)

Canada
Canadian Equestrian Federation
1600 James Naismith Drive
Gloucester
Ontario
Canada
LOA 1BO

Canadian Dressage Owners and
Riders Association Inc.
(CADORA Inc.)
RR 1, Campbellcroft
Ontario
Canada
LOA 1BO

Canadian Pony Club Association
11B Laidlaw Blvd
Markham

Ontario
Canada
L3P 1W5
(131 branches.)

Great Britain
The British Horse Society
The Dressage Group
British Equestrian Centre
Stoneleigh
Kenilworth
Warwickshire
CV8 2LR

The Pony Club
British Equestrian Centre
Stoneleigh
Kenilworth
Warwickshire
CV8 2LR
(367 branches in Great Britain and
in 25 other countries. This Pony
Club is the parent of all Pony
Clubs and is the headquarters of
the Pony Club for the world.
Information can be obtained
about branches worldwide from
this address.)

Ireland
Equestrian Federation of Ireland
Anglesea Lodge
Anglesea Rd.
Ballsbridge
Dublin 4
Ireland

The Irish Dressage Committee
Mrs Joan Keogh
Spruce Lodge
Kilternan
Co. Dublin
Ireland

Irish Pony Club Advisory Board
Sec. Mrs P. Riall
Knocbawn
Likmacanogue
Co. Cork
Ireland
(42 branches.)

New Zealand
New Zealand Horse Society Inc.
P.O. Box 47
Hastings
Hawkes Bay
New Zealand

New Zealand Pony Clubs
Association
Sec. Mrs J. Wakeling
Kaitieke
RD2 Owhango
New Zealand
(82 branches.)

South Africa
South African Equestrian
Federation
P.O. Box 69414
Bryanston 2021
South Africa RSA

South African Pony Club
National Committee
Sec. Mrs C. Packham
9 Roxburghe Avenue
Craighall Park
Johannesburg 2196
South Africa

United States of America
American Horse Shows
Association Inc.
220 East 42nd Street
Fourth Floor
New York
N Y 10017-5806
USA

United States Pony Clubs Inc.
Contact: Susan Giddings,
National Administration
893 S. Matlack St, Suite 110,
West Chester
PA 19382 - 4913
USA
(431 clubs.)

United States Dressage
Federation Inc.
1212 O Street
PO Box 80668
Lincoln
Nebraska 80668
USA

Index

Page numbers in *italic* indicate illustrations